Fishing Tackle
MADE IN MISSOURI
History and Identification

by Dean A. Murphy

DAMMO Publishing Company
7076 North Shore Drive
Hartsburg, MO 65039

FOREWORD

Collectors are collectors because they enjoy finding and possessing the items. Fishing tackle collectors combine the enjoyment of collecting with the sport of fishing.

Anyone who engages in a concerted research effort does so for the inherent intrigue of the search and the love of knowledge for its own sake. Many people enjoy the research but it takes a special individual to put the results in writing and share it with others.

One such person is Dean Murphy of Hartsburg, Missouri. His love of the out-of-doors and of history provided a combination of interests and talents that suited him well in developing a "genealogy of Missouri fishing tackle." Dean told me he started with Pflueger but after a while needed a new direction for his collecting. He found this direction in collecting fishing tackle made in Missouri.

Dean started research on Missouri tackle in about 1989. The more he learned, the more he got caught up in the search for new information. One contact led to another and each new piece of information filled a gap in the historical account. His research convinced him that the history of Missouri's fishing tackle heritage needed to be documented and that time was running out on opportunities to obtain first or even second hand information. Indeed, this generation, and the knowledge only it possesses, is quickly passing from us to be lost forever. The culmination of Dean Murphy's dedicated efforts is this book, "Fishing Tackle Made in Missouri: History and Identification."

I hope others will be stimulated by the example set forth by Dean and will get about the urgent task of researching and documenting the history of fishing tackle and companies of their respective interests and states. Generations to come will acknowledge their valiant efforts as they read with joy the development of their hobby, collecting old fishing tackle.

Those of us in Missouri and elsewhere thank you, Dean Murphy, for your contribution to the recorded history of the fishing tackle industry.

Thomas R. Yonke
Columbia, Missouri

ACKNOWLEDGEMENTS

Many fishing tackle collectors from Missouri contributed to this project and I gratefully recognize their generous assistance in locating and securing many of the examples illustrated. They were: Archie Allen, Bill Calhoun, Don Getz, Kermit Gohring, Ollie Hibbler, Jeff Kieny, Dennis Lane, Frank Lewis, Allen McCord, Jery McLean, Dudley Murphy, Henry Norris, Warren Platt, Art Province, Kevin Richards, Larry Ross, Charles Sanders, Dale Thomas, Michael Williams and Tom Yonke. My apologies to anyone I have overlooked. Jack Looney, Steve White and Dan Wyatt deserve special credit.

Bill Bennitt, Roger Moore, Dick Rotsch, Herb Schwartz and Joel Vance provided leads to valuable sources of information. Thanks, fellows.

Individual lure makers or their families provided information and materials. This project would have been impossible without their help, and I gratefully acknowledge their contributions. Credit will be given in the text of the appropriate company.

Credit is due to Larry Smith for furnishing copies of early advertisements, and to Dick Streater for permission to reproduce advertisements from his book.

Tom Yonke and Charles Davidson reviewed the manuscript and provided editorial comment. Their advice is appreciated.

I am especially grateful to my daughter, Cathleen Murphy, for lay-out and preparation of the manuscript. My wife, Bette, deserves special recognition for her support and tolerance during this effort.

TABLE OF CONTENTS

Introduction

Chronology of Fishing Tackle Made in Missouri

Before 1900...1
1900 through 1929 1
1930 through 1943 6
1944 through 1963 16
1964 through 1989 34

Information Needed 40

Homemade 46

Companies in Business-1992 51

Early Distributors 52

Patents Issued to Missourians 55

References 109

Index 110

**Missouri Center
for the Book**

𕞥𕞥𕞥

**Missouri Authors
Collection**

INTRODUCTION

My intent in writing this book is to present a historical record of all fishing tackle made in Missouri. I have not restricted myself to lures, rods, and reels, but have included all tackle. Information from the earliest records to the contemporary are included. I chose to include all tackle and contemporary items because collecting fishing tackle is a relatively new hobby, and future collectors may value the identification of the later items.

I believe that we must gather all pertinent information while it is still available. Many of the people I interviewed were quite elderly and at least one has died since the interview. The records of their companies will soon be lost.

Readers will notice several companies with a Kansas address. My reasoning is that Kansas City, Kansas, is actually a part of metropolitan Kansas City.

Some of the books listed in the Reference Section give suggested values for lures. I have not set values because they change rapidly with current demands.

The size of lures is given to aid in identification. The length given is the length of the body, exclusive of hook hangers, propellors, or diving lips.

CHRONOLOGY OF FISHING TACKLE MADE IN MISSOURI

The earliest fishing tackle company in Missouri was the Lutz Pork Bait Company which began in 1890. The first company to market a fishing lure was the Charmer Minnow Company, which began around 1910.

Before 1900

The first reference to fishing tackle in Missouri was Patent No. 185,914 issued to A. H. Gregg of St. Louis in 1877. The patent was for "an artificial hook-bait of rubber or other suitable flexible material made in form and color to imitate the ordinary earth-worm." Two other patents were issued to Missourians prior to 1900 (see Patent Section). No examples have been found of the products illustrated in these early patents.

Lutz Pork Bait Company
920 and 924 Wyandotte
Kansas City

LUTZ

Assorted Color Pork Rind Strips; Equal Amount of Green and White and Red and White; Glistening White Makes it Easily Seen for a Considerable Distance Even in Murky Water; its Wiggle Makes it Look Like a Live Minnow; Tough and Leathery, Hard to Tear; Twelve Strips, Four Assorted Colors, in an Air Tight Glass Container.

Per Dozen Jars
No. LPB—Weight per Dozen Jars, 6¾ lbs. $10.80
One Dozen Jars in a Carton

The company was started by Frank Lutz. It began business in 1890 and continued for over 75 years. Lutz was the first company to sell an artificial bait in Missouri. Patent No. 2,501,449 was issued March 21, 1950, to A. S. & H. J. Lutz. The patent was for a chunk-type,

pork rind bait. Five trademarks representing different styles of pork rind were registered in 1951. The company was in business until the late 1960s. At that time, MarLynn Lure Company bought the rights to the Boomerang spinner bait and Weber Company bought the pork rind business.

1900 through 1929

Arnold Manufacturing Company
2328 A Brooklyn
Kansas City

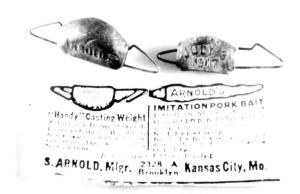

Sigel Arnold owner. Lead casting weight, patented July 3, 1917, Patent No. 1,232,167. Artificial pork rind patented July 19, 1918, Patent No. 1,272,183. The company was in business from 1917 until at least 1927, according to an advertisement in Streater (p. 11).

Charmer Minnow Company
Springfield

Charmer Minnow - 3 1/4"

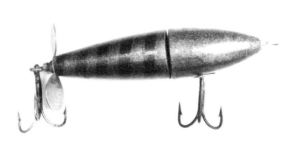

Surface Charmer - 3 1/2"

F. W. Breder and J. H. Loyd owners. Patent No. 972,748 for the Charmer Minnow was issued to Breder and Loyd on Nov. 11, 1910. Loyd assigned his portion of the patent to Marshall O. Brixey, Springfield. Another patent, Reissue No. 13,499, for the Surface Charmer was issued to them on Dec. 12, 1912. They apparently began producing the Charmer Minnow sometime before 1910.

The company also made a limited number of Midget Charmers (2 5/8") and Musky Charmers (5"). For a more detailed discussion of the Charmer Minnow Company see *The Barberpole Baits,* by Bill Calhoun, National Fishing Lure Collectors Club (NFLCC) Magazine, July, 1991.

Diamond Manufacturing Company
St. Louis

Diamond Manufacturing Company was the manufacturing branch of Shapleigh Hardware. Some early spinners bear the initials, N. S. H. Co., meaning Norvell-Shapleigh Hardware Company. The name was changed to Shapleigh Hardware in 1929. I do not know whether they actually made the tackle or assembled it from purchased components. Diamond Brand, Mizzoo, Triumph, Ultra (lines) and Hinduvine (fly rods) were some of their registered trademarks. The company went out of business in 1959.

Fisherman's Supply Company
796 Aubert Ave.
St. Louis

An article by Larry Smith in The N.F.L.C.C. Gazette (December, 1991) showed an advertisement from 1919. Fisherman's Supply

1919 — MAGNO PREPARED BAIT

GET AHEAD OF THE GAME
OUR NEVER-FAIL-ANGLER
will enable you to catch
more fish than ever. Try
one, they are of the
greatest value to fisher-
men. We are the origi-
nators of MAGNO PREPARED BAIT, a scientific
compound which has proven it's worth. Ever ready for
use, beats them all, it's so convenient. Sample size box 25c. Full
size box 50c. Send for our circulars of trap nets, hooks, etc.
FISHERMAN'S SUPPLY CO., 796 Aubert Ave.,   ST. LOUIS, MO.

Courtesy Larry Smith

Company made and marketed a "scientific compound" called Magno Prepared Bait. The advertisement also included their "never-fail-angler," a baited, collapsing net which was suspended below the water's surface by means of a float.

J. F. Gregory
St. Louis, Kansas City

Courtesy Larry Smith

Larry Smith in the N.F.L.C.C. Gazette (December, 1991) reported Magic Fish Lure was first marketed in 1912, and was undoubtedly a financial success because Gregory promoted it nationally for many years.

The wooden box in the photograph contains a white powder. The label says, "To one ounce

of this preparation add one ounce of sweet oil." J. F. Gregory and Company, Kansas City, was issued a trademark on April 15, 1952. Did Gregory move to Kansas City and continue in business into the 1950s?

Magnetic Fish Bait Company
Republic

The only information is a 1910 ad shown in Smith, p.39.

Courtesy Larry Smith

Missouri Bait Company
St. Louis

Produced the Mizzouri Bug Wabler (2") which was patented May 23, 1916, according to the metal plate on the lure. Patent No. 1,184,588

3

Perfection Bait Company
16 E. 11th
Kansas City

Courtesy Larry Smith

The only information is the advertisement in Smith, p.99.

was issued on May 23, 1916, to William J. Sprague of Kansas City. An advertisement in Streater (p. 12B) is dated 1923, which indicates the company was in business for several years.

Naturalure Company
2606 Olive St.
Kansas City

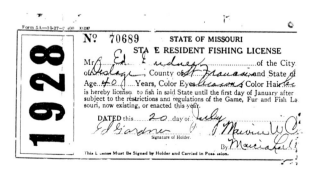

Owned by Bert Mayfield. The 1929 catalog indicates that the company was in business during the 1920s. The company was purchased by MarLynn Lure Company in 1953.

Thanks to Ted Green.

Self-Striking Fish Cork Company
St. Louis

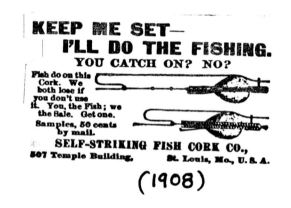

Courtesy Dick Streater

An advertisement for this product is shown in Streater, p.212A. It is dated 1908.

William H. Talbot Reel Company
122 Washington Street
Nevada

William H. Talbot was a watch-maker in Nevada, Missouri. He apparently started making reels about 1900, because he received Patent No. 666,398 on January 22, 1901. The patent was for the three screw front plate, which characterized his reels.

William H. Talbot Reel Company was incorporated November 11, 1904, by W. H. Talbot, E. E. Levens, H. M. Duck, and J. J. Stockard. The address for the corporation was changed to Kansas City in September, 1913. The name of the company was changed to William H. Talbot Reel and Manufacturing Company in October, 1913. The company was dissolved in 1924.

Early Talbot reels were advertised as being available in brass, German silver and sterling silver. The most expensive Talbot reels were "fully jeweled" and featured "S" curved handles. They were identified by number. Less expensive reels were marked "Nevada" and "Kansas City."

Talbot continued making reels until 1914 and retired from the company in 1916. The company was purchased by the Richardson Rod and Reel company of Chicago shortly after World War I.

J. A. Wavrin
3156 South Grand Avenue
St. Louis

Courtesy Larry Smith

The only information is a 1919 advertisement for a rubber pork rind shown in Smith (p.81).

Clinton Wilt Manufacturing Company
331 North Campbell
Springfield

Wilt Champion- 3 1/4"

Little Wonder- 2 1/4"

Clinton Wilt owned a coal and ice company. Patent No.1,073,199 was issued to Wilt on September 16, 1913. It was for the Little Wonder lure. The application was filed in 1911, but he probably began making lures before that time. Very little is known about the Wilt Company. For a more detailed discussion of what is known, see *The Barberpole Baits*, by Bill Calhoun (NFLCC Magazine, July, 1991).

C. A. Clark Company
218 1/2 West Walnut Street
Springfield

Popper Scout - 2 1/2"

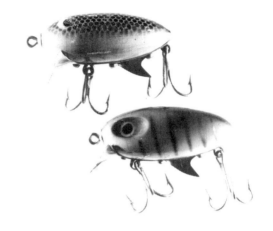

Water Scout- painted eye
Water Scout - indented eye

Little Eddie - 1 3/4"
Dwarf Deamon - 2"

Jointed Scout - 2 3/4"
Top Darter Scout - 3"

Experimental Lure - 3"
Goofy Gus - 3"

Duckbill - 2 1/4"
Duckling - 2"

C.A. Clark Company (cont'd)

Top: Water Scout - dent eye - 2 1/4"
Middle; Water Scout-carved eye - 2 1/4"
Bottom: Streamliner - 2"

Ser. No. 400,589. CHARLES A. CLARK, doing business as C. A. Clark Co., Springfield, Mo. Filed Dec. 8, 1937.

WATER SCOUT

For Artificial Bait.
Claims use since June, 1935.

Charles A. Clark was issued Patent No. 1,981,091 for the Water Scout on November 20, 1934. There is some evidence that he began producing the lure before that time. Trademark 400,589 was registered April 12, 1938. Ike Six remembers Mr. Clark as a very tall and thin man.

Brochures and boxes indicate the first name was C. A. Clark Company, followed by C. A. Clark Manufacturing Company, and finally Water Scout Company. Incorporation records give an indication as to the timing of these changes. C. A. Clark Manufacturing Company

was incorporated January 23, 1947, by Charles A., Edgar C., and Marie C. Clark. Charles and Edgar were given as partners. The name was changed to C. A. Clark, Inc. on April 6, 1953. Only C. A. and Marie Clark are listed as shareholders. The incorporation was forfeited January 16, 1954, for failing to file required annual reports. The petition for reinstatement listed C. A. Clark, Frank C. Mann, and Marie C. Clark. Mr. Mann was an attorney in Springfield. The corporation was revoked January 1, 1959. There was no mention of the Water Scout Company in the incorporation files.

The Water Scout was the first lure Clark produced. There were several variations in hardware, body shape, and eye design but it continued through the life of the company. Water Scout, Popper Scout, Little Eddie, Dwarf Deamon, Goofy Gus and early models of Duckbill and Duckling were all wooden lures. Streamliner, Darter/Top Scout and Jointed Scout were Tenite.

For an in-depth discussion of the lures produced by the company see *"The Water Scout and Other Clark Baits"* ,by Jim Barzee and Jim Bourdon.

E. E. Coombs
3816 Wyoming
Kansas City

Courtesy Larry Smith

Information on this company is limited to a 1940(?) advertisement shown in Smith, p. 139, and two lures illustrated in White (2nd Ed., p.149, D6 & D7). The lure was made of Catalin, an early plastic. The lures were 2 3/4" and 1 3/4".

F. B. Cravens Lures
Golden City

Fremont Beck Cravens was a WWI veteran and optometrist. His wife, Isa, tied the flies and he made the popping bugs. Beck Cravens also was an artist who created paintings of dogs and scenery. The paintings and lures were sold during summer auto trips throughout the United States. They were in business for only 3 or 4 years in the 1930s.

Thanks to Mrs. F. B. Cravens.

Culver Lure Company
3227 Missouri Avenue
St. Louis

Owned by Harry Sims. Advertisements in 1930s hunting and fishing magazines offered a free catalog of fly and rod making supplies. Company was still in business in 1960.

Gilmore Tackle Company
(Natural Fly Company)
Windsor

Basil Eugene Gilmore, owner. Patent No. 2,473,142 issued June 14, 1949, was for a sponge-rubber, flyrod lure. Gilmore began tying flies in Kansas City, but went to Windsor in l937. He lived in the country south of town and hired neighbor women to tie flies. The Gillie flies were advertised in national magazines as early as 1938.

His first shop was upstairs in what is presently the Western Auto building in Windsor. Some of the women from the country worked for him there. He built a building at 103 Florence Street in 1946, and employed about 20 people. The name change from Gilmore Tackle Company to Natural Fly Company occurred prior to the move to the new building. Gilmore died in 1967, but his widow continued the business until 1984.

Natural Fly Company produced a line of fiberglass rods in addition to flies and poppers. One rod, the Wee Jigger, was especially popular with crappie fishermen and is in demand today, if you can find one. The 4 1/2 foot rod was turned (underwater) to a diameter smaller than a lead pencil, and was sensitive to the lightest bite.

Like many of the early lure makers, Gilmore was an innovator. He had a secret glue which he made by dissolving movie film in acetate. He perfected a machine to saw the groove for the hook and adapted dentist drills to round the rear and hollow the heads of his poppers. He lined the bowl of an old cream separator with sandpaper and attached a motor. The cork bodies for his poppers were tumbled in this drum.

Thanks to Mrs. Basil Gilmore and Bob Moss.

Bill Herington Bait Company
Green City

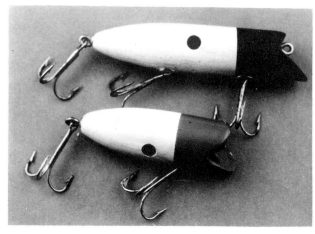

Bag-O-Mad - 3 3/4"
Bag-O-Mad Jr. - 2 3/4"

Experimental Bag-O-Mad - 3"

Ser. No. 334,838.   W. A. HERINGTON, Green City, Mo.
Filed Feb. 10, 1933.

BAG-O-MAD

For Fish Lure or Artificial Bait.
Claims use since July 1, 1932.

William A. (Bill) Herington, owner. Patent No. 1,854,696 for the Bag-O-Mad lure issued on April 19, 1932. Trademark 334,838 was registered April 11, 1933. Herington was a teacher/coach at Trenton Junior College, Trenton, Missouri, from 1930 to 1937. He was a coach (basketball and baseball) at Culver Stockton College, Canton, Missouri, from 1938 until his death in 1965. His father was a doctor in Green City, and Bill stayed with him

in the summer and produced the lures in a workshop.

Bodies for the lures were purchased from a company in Ohio. The lures were painted by dipping, which explains the relatively poor paint job and the often irregular line between head and body colors.

He was in the business for about 5 years (1932-1937). The lures were advertised in national magazines, sold in local stores, and distributed by a sporting goods company in Kansas City. The business was sold to the Kansas City company in about 1941. Mrs. Herington thought the company may have been Elliot Arms.

Carol Russell was an assistant coach and friend of Herington. He said the lure was a real bass catcher, but was too large for the preference of local fishermen. Russell recalls going with Herington to pick up some lures he had on consignment at a sporting goods store in Kansas City. The store owner's excuse for not having sold the lures was, "the three treble hooks were unfair to the fish".

Thanks to Mrs. Leo Herington, Donna Herington, and Carol Russell.

**Litton Tackle Company
821 North Mill St.
Festus**

**McDonald Manufacturing Company
P. O. Box 7
Lee's Summit**

Howard C. Litton was a teacher and high school guidance counselor. He became an avid fisherman after a vacation with friends at the Lake of the Ozarks in the late 1930s. The Irresistible lure was developed during the early 1940s. Litton found a lady who was a professional flie tyer and hired her to make his products.

Litton's Irresistible was a lead-headed lure with a round lip. It came in 12 colors, some of which were named for favorite color patterns of his fishing buddies. The jig, without the lip, was sold in combination with several types of spinners. Other products included flies, weighted flies and line dressing. Linotype metal was used for the lead-heads because it held paint better than plain lead. There were no patents or trademarks.

His products were not sold through wholesalers or advertised in publications, but were sold personally by Litton on week-end trips through eastern Missouri. He conducted the business as a hobby. When it grew to the point of forcing a decision to teach or go into business full-time, he chose teaching. Howard Litton died in the fall of 1992.

Thanks to Howard Litton.

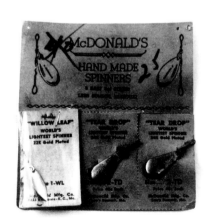

Donald D. McDonald owned a jewelry store in Kansas City from 1927 to 1945 and in Lee's Summit from 1945 to 1949. McDonald Manufacturing was famous for its flyrod spinners, which were actually gold plated. The name was changed to McDonald Manufacturers and Importers at an unknown date.

Trademark 581,716, registered October 27, 1953, assigned the Lif-Lik Lure trademark to McDonald. A variety of soft plastic lures were marketed under the McDonald Lif-Lik label. McDonald died in 1990 at the age of 86.

May Fly Company
510 Benton
Monett

Joe W. May, owner. Joe May owned a produce and moving business in Illinois. According to family tradition, he was forced to close it because of an unfortunate investment in a boxcar full of eggs. He moved to Monett and went to work for the Midwest Map Company. May had begun tying flies in the 1920s and by 1931, the demand for his flies had become sufficient for him to quit Midwest Map and go into business as The May Fly Company. The company produced woolyworm flies, popping bugs and a bait called "Spineree." The office-workshop occupied a large garage behind May's house.

May had no patents or registered trademarks, but Ike Six thought he may have invented the woolyworm fly. Six also said May frequently fished Roaring River State Park. May's family said he was a tremendous trout fisherman.

The flies were packaged in cellophane bags and stapled to display cards. They were sold locally, and were wholesaled to state parks, and to Sears and Roebuck stores in Springfield, Joplin and Kansas City. They also may have been sold at Wal-Mart in the early years of that company. May company went out of business in 1980, and Joe May died in 1982 at the age of 96.

Thanks to Max May.

Natural Fly Company
Windsor

(See Gilmore Tackle Company)

The Ozark Bait Company
California

Herman G. Swearingen, California, Missouri, received Patent No. 1,812,906 on July 7, 1931. He assigned one-fourth of the patent to H. R. Popejoy and one-fourth to J. R. Popejoy, both of California. Swearingen was a welder who lived north of McGirk. H. R. Popejoy was a doctor. His son, J. R. Popejoy, was a dentist. The Popejoys financed the patenting of the lure invented by Swearingen.

He carved the prototype out of wood but the lure in the picture is cast aluminum. It is called The Sheik (3"). Spring-loaded hooks for the interior of the lure never were produced commercially. Mrs. Swearingen said that her husband made a prototype by clipping off the head and point of a safety pin and soldering long shank hooks to it.

The partners had a falling-out and in December, 1930, Swearingen filed a suit with the courts to prevent the Popejoys from marketing the lure without due compensation to him. The lure was apparently never marketed.

Thanks to Mrs. Herman Swearingen.

J. R. Plasters
(Division of Laskers Steel)
22 W. 800 Terrace
J. R. Plasters
3600 E. 55th St.
Kansas City

Manufactured Ideal trot line clips and cottonseed bait holders for trot lines. James R. Plaster received two patents for fish stringers, No. 1,975,864 on October 9, 1934, and No. 2,047,834 on July 14, 1936. I have been told the company produced the stringers but have found no examples. The company was sold to Noel A. Price who continues to market the trot-line clips and cottonseed holders under the NAPCO brand.

Split Cork Float
Springfield

This cork was patented by a Dr. Craig, probably in the early 1930s, according to Bill Calhoun. Dr. Craig was a fishing buddy of Stanley Myers (Springfield Novelty Company).

Springfield Novelty Company
631 South Broadway
Springfield

Lead headed Reel Lure - 3"
Early Reel Lure - 2"

Stanley F. Myers worked for Southwestern Bell Telephone Company. Adolph Kunz operated a machine shop. They became fishing buddies after Kunz repaired Myers' favorite reel in the late 1920s. They received Patent No. 1,931,932 for the Reel Lure on October 24, 1933.

Kunz had previously worked for the Charmer Minnow Company. He apparently had a supply of the rear section of Charmer Minnows, and these were used in making the first Reel Lures. Bill Calhoun thinks that these lures should be called the 1/2 Charmer. Myers apparently was the "idea" man, while Kunz had the mechanical ability to design the equipment for making the lures. Their business was housed in the garage behind

Myers' home. The two men and their sons made the lures during off-hours from their regular jobs.

The earliest lures were packaged in white boxes with red borders, and had a picture of the lure on the top. The boxes were changed to solid red when the Heddon company claimed the originals too closely resembled their box. Later Reel Lures had a coil of wire in front of the rear hook, apparently to keep the hook from fouling. An experimental musky size lure was produced in very limited numbers. A lure with a lead nose ahead of the rotating rear body was called the 1/2 Charmer by some authors. Bill Calhoun calls it the Hollowhead. It also was produced in limited numbers because it too closely resembled the Charmer lure.

The company continued only until 1935 when Kunz became ill. Stanley Myers died in 1991. My file card indicates Kunz and Myers also patented a fish stringer.

Stanley Myers became an honorary member of the NFLCC in 1989 (NFLCC Gazette, September, 1989). For further details on the company, see *The Barberpole Lures, Part Two*, by Bill Calhoun (NFLCC Magazine, March, 1992).

Howard W. Steen (& Sons.) Doniphan

Howard Steen was raised in Goose Hollow, about 2 miles from the Current River in Carter

county. He began tying flies in 1923, but didn't start selling them until 1933. He received Patent No. 2,532,961 on February 5, 1950. It was for a method of making double flies. The fly in the lower left of the photo is his double fly. The flies on the lower right are prepared for his method of tying in a trailer-hook.

His first addresses were Grandin and Van Buren. He moved to Doniphan in 1946. His products were sold by taking sample cards of his flies to stores in Missouri, Arkansas, Illinois, and Kansas. He would tie the flies that had been ordered and mail them to the retailer in a flat, red box.

In addition to flies, Steen also made lead-head lures, poppers and a few wooden lures. The lure in the photograph is 2 ". He also built and repaired fishing rods and repaired reels. Mr. Steen is in his mid 80s and still lives in Doniphan.

Thanks to Mrs. Leona Steen, Ronnie Steen, Henry Norris and Loren Randall.

Taneycomo Fish Bait Company
Branson

Dellas J. Spence received Patent No. 1,795,238 on May 19, 1928. The patent was for a dough bait mixture. A trademark published May 19, 1931, said, "Dellas J. Spence doing business as Taneycomo Fish Bait Company." The trademark was TAN-CO-MO. A bait called

Ser. No. 312,393. DELLAS J. SPENCE, doing business as Taneycomo Fish Bait Company, Branson, Mo. Filed Mar. 21, 1931.

TAN-CO-MO

For Prepared Fish Bait.
Claims use since Mar. 15, 1926.

"Laverix" was advertised in the 1939 catalog of Richards and Conover Hardware Company, Kansas City, which indicates the company was in business until at least 1939.

Walter C. Taylor
St. Louis

Taylor received Patent No. 1,583,199 for a flyrod popper on May 4, 1926. He apparently assigned the patent to Peckinpaugh company, which produced the Peck-Taylor frog.

1944 through 1963

This time period was chosen because the Postal Service used numbers to divide large cities into zones from May, 1944, to July, 1963. Therefore, it is possible to date some companies by their address.

Anderson Bait Company
Springfield

Owner unknown. Patent applied for. Trademark was ABC Bait. This very colorful plastic bait came in a yellow cardboard box. An advertisement shown in Streater (p. 12) is dated 1949, and helps to establish the time frame for the company.

AR-CO-MO Company
Branson

Harold Epps owned the Western Auto store and Bob Curry owned a lumberyard in the early 1950s, when they formed the AR-CO-MO company. The name stood for Arkansas, Missouri country. They made two topwater lures, the Hornet Sr. (2 3/4") and the Hornet JR. (1 3/4"). According to Epps, they also made two other lures. Bodies for the Hornet lures were made in Branson, and were painted by Roy Dodgen at the School of the Ozarks.

The lures were packaged in plastic boxes and sold at local tackle stores in south central Missouri and in Kansas City, where they were advertised and endorsed by Harold Ensley. They were very popular during the first years at Bull Shoals Lake. This popularity faded quickly, and the company was in business for only 2 years.

Harold Epps worked as a guide for Jim Owens during his teen-age years, and remembers Captain Dave Hawk (Hawk Lure Company) as a frequent customer. He said Hawk was a big guy who always wore a ship captains cap.

Thanks to Harold Epps.

B & F Manufacturing Company
Rolla

J. J. (Jim) Fuller was one of five brothers raised in Cuba, Missouri. Jim lived in Sullivan for awhile and moved to Rolla in the 1930s. He was a jeweler-watchmaker by trade, but was involved in many other projects. Among his inventions was a device which raised a flag when a postman placed letters in a rural mailbox.

His most successful business was the manufacture and sale of the High-Striker. This device is the familiar carnival game where a person tries to ring a bell at the top of a tall pole by hitting a lever with a large mallet.

He ventured into fishing lure manufacturing and sales around 1960. The plastic lures, of at least six designs, were made in his basement. They were packaged in plastic boxes and most were sold locally. The brand name was Bass-in-Net. Fuller was in the lure business for only two or three years. Bill Wright bought the business and later sold it to someone in the Lake of the Ozarks area.

Thanks to Jim Hatchett.

Baker's Impy Lure Company
824 N. Kansas
Marceline

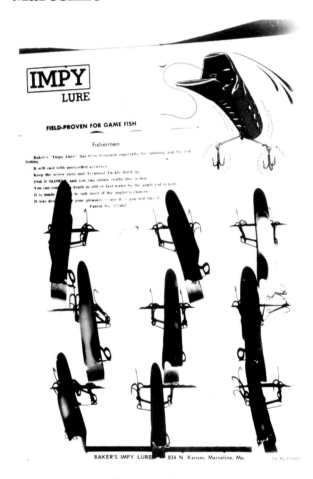

Paul Baker, owner. Patent No. 2,775,841 was issued to Baker on January 1, 1957. No

trademark. Baker was a conductor on the Santa Fe railroad until he retired in 1958. He distributed the lures by traveling throughout Missouri and putting the lures on consignment at appropriate businesses. They were not advertised or sold by mail. Lures were packaged in plastic bags and mounted on cardboard displays. The first lures were molded of polyethylene, but they would not hold paint. The marketed lures were molded of poly-styrene and were painted by Berry-Lebeck Company. The lures came in two sizes, 2 " and 2 1/2".

Thanks to Paul Baker.

Berry-Lebeck Manufacturing Company
320 South High Street
California

Talky-Topper - 3"

Wood Wee Gee - 2 1/2"

Paul Lebeck owned and operated a cabinet shop. The company was located in his shop. Robert Berry was a salesman for Wohl Shoe Company. His territory included Iowa, Minnesota, and North Dakota. He used his travels to promote the lures and collect bad debts. Lebeck produced the lures and filled the orders.

Berry applied on November 1, 1945, but did not receive Patent No. 2,510,769 until June 6, 1950. The patent was for the Talky-Topper lure and it featured the "no foul" tail clip, which prevents the rear hook from swinging forward. The no foul clip is a distinguishing feature of Berry-Lebeck lures. "Ozarka Lure" was their trademark.

The Talky-Topper, designated the 100 Series, was the first lure produced. It was an excellent topwater bait, and was endorsed by noted fisherman-writer, Robert Page Lincoln. The wooden bodies were supplied by a St. Louis company. Several attempts were made to develop a plastic (Tenite) Talky-Topper, but they were not successful.

The wooden Wee Gee, designated the 200 Series, resembled a Schmoo. It apparently was produced for only a short period of time. Unsuccessful attempts also were made to produce it in plastic. A wooden prototype indicates they thought of producing a crawdad type lure using the wooden Wee Gee body.

A plastic Wee Gee, designated the 300 Series, was developed and marketed. This lure has been mis-identified in earlier editions of other reference books, probably because it is frequently found in Talky-Topper boxes.

The company also produced a horsehide reel case with a zipper, stamped Ozarka Lure Reel Case. It came in three colors.

Berry-Lebeck products were advertised in all the major magazines and were sold throughout the United States. They also had a very active distributor in Canada. Western Auto stores were a major retailer. The business closed following Berry's death in 1951.

Thanks to Paul Lebeck and Ron Drury.

Cal Biddlecome Bait Manufacturing Company
Cal Biddlecome Fly Company
Carthage

Cal Biddlecome owned and operated Biddlecome Fly Company, probably in the 1940s.

Cal's Crippled Minnow-3 3/4"

He was in business with Ike Six for a short time around 1950. He made and sold several lures under his own name after he left the Six company.

Plastic Wee Gee 2"

Biddlecome-Six Tackle Company
Carthage

(See Charles M. Six Tackle Company)

Carnival Cork Company
4077 Fillmore
St. Louis

Incorporated June 27, 1963, by John Hubatchek.

Central Molding and
Manufacturing Company
1509 Central
Kansas City

Made a plastic, egg-shaped float called the Bomb. The brand name for the company was Philson. They also made an aluminum tackle box which was advertised in Outdoor Life, May, 1955.

Century Plastic Company
1616 Chestnut St.
St. Louis

Made Gee Gee Glow Worm, a twisted stick of plastic that was luminous after exposure to light. Incorporated September 15, 1947, by Theodore Waxman and Harry Gardner. Copyrighted in 1949.

Courtney Specialty Company
31st Street around Prospect
Kansas City

Les Courtney and Ed Moore were co-owners of the company. They had no patents or trademarks. Made the Deep Diver, a lead-headed, rubber skirted bait with a nose spinner.

McDonald Manufacturing Company apparently bought the rights to the Deep Diver, because it also was marketed by them.

Thanks to Roger Moore.

D. B. Doty, Inc.
Columbia

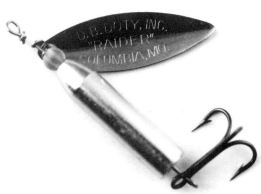

Falcon Products
2910 Washington Avenue
St. Louis

Incorporated December 20, 1957 by Donald P. Gallop. It was merged with a Delaware corporation on December 2, 1974. They made jigs and spinner baits.

W. W. Faris Manufacturing Company
St. Louis

Dabney B. Doty was a professor at the University of Missouri. Trademark "Raider" registered in Missouri only. Doty developed the Raider lure in 1949-50. His objective was to make a lure that would catch more fish than the lures used by his fishing buddies Joe Jonakin and George Braloe. The Raider was so successful that the three men formed the company in 1951 and continued until 1980.

Thanks to Dabney Doty.

Began as Faris and Smith Plastic Flooring Company in 1942. The name was changed to W. W. Faris Company on December 13, 1945. Incorporation was revoked February 29, 1960. Company was listed in the 1948 Sporting Goods Dealers Directory.

Fetchi Popeye - 3"

This company and the FlexiLure company were operated by the Southwest Distributors, which was owned by Fred R. and Albert Harris. Fetchi Lure Company was incorporated September 20, 1954. Southwest Distributors was changed to Dehyco Company, January 20, 1965.

**Fetchi Lure Company
2026 Broadway
Kansas City**

**Flexilure Company
Kansas City**

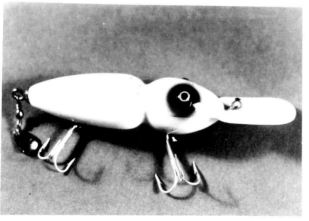

Fetchi Lizard - 4"

(See Fetchi Lure Company) Flexilure Company was incorporated April 12, 1954. The soft plastic minnow produced by this company is almost identical to the Merry Minnow of the McDonald Manufacturing Company.

H & K Sales Company
4327 Troost
Kansas City

Incorporated September 17, 1954, by Robert W. Weary, L. T. Reinhoet, and Edwin J. Corry. The incorporation was revoked February 28, 1984. Henry Norris reported that this company made and sold a wire line snap called the Henson Hitch.

Hawk Fish Lure Corporation
1651 South Grand Avenue
St. Louis

Incorporated November 17, 1948, by Clyde W. Bailey, Olan L. Hawk and D. J. Bolfing. The address of Olan Hawk at the time of incorporation was Ardmore, Oklahoma. Included in the assets of the new corporation were "all of the assets and liabilities of a former business operated by one of the incorporators, Olan L. Hawk." It seems that the Hawk Lure Company originated in Oklahoma, but what was the company name in Oklahoma? Company literature referred to Olan Hawk as "the famous Captain Hawk".

The Bayou Boogie (2 1/2 " & 1 1/2"), Fly Boogie and Topper lures were marketed by the A. D. Manufacturing Company, a Division of Hawk Lure Company. Bayou Boogie lures were also sold by the Whopper Stopper Bait Company of Texas. What is the relationship?

The Hawk Lure Company was sold to a man named Brown from St. Louis, date unknown. Hawk lures are found in boxes with a California address, indicating that the company may have moved.

Dave Hawk, the Captain's son, had a tackle manufacturing business in Harrisonville, Arkansas, in the early 1950s. He sold the business to MarLynn Lure Company in 1955, and became a fishing guide in Matzelan, Mexico.

Mike Hildreth
Jacksonville

Top: Bass Hawk - 1 3/8"
Bottom: Bombadier - 1 5/8"

Mike Hildreth came to Missouri in 1934. He had traded a grapefruit orchard in Edenburg, Texas, for a farm south of Jacksonville. A brochure in the lure box says that Hildreth got the idea for the lure while on a trip to old Mexico in 1927. His son, Chuck, says the lure (2 1/2") was modeled after a big locust which swarmed annually in southern Texas. Hildreth's children carved and made the lures during winters on the farm, and sold them for spending money the next summer.

Hildreth moved to Colorado in 1963, and was in the mining business. He established a small factory with 3-5 workers and went into commercial production of the lure. He loaded the first 10,000 in a pickup truck and drove to Texas, where he sold them all. The business lasted 4 to 5 years. Mike Hildreth died in Midway, Arkansas in 1979.

Thanks to Chuck Hildreth.

Houser Fly Company
St. Louis

Paul Houser received Patent No. 2,564,260 for a trotline hook on August 14, 1951. He started in business at 924 Kingshighway in the early 1930s. The family lived in the rear of the building. There was a shop in front and a workshop in the middle. He employed three women to tie flies. Around 1940, he bought 926 Kingshighway, and expanded the business. He sold a general line of sporting goods, but specialized in fishing tackle. His motto was

"Lose a little on each sale but make it up on volume." A warehouse was added to the rear of the property in 1947, at which time Houser bought a jack-chain machine and began manufacturing stringers. The area became known as "the chain yard". He employed 10 people at the peak of the business. The business was dissolved in 1971, and sold to MarLynn Lure Company, Kansas City, in 1974. Paul Houser died in 1976.

Houser always claimed to have invented the single-spin bait, but apparently never patented it. His Helldiver was one of the first single-spins. Houser was reported to have caught large bass, tattooed on their cheek "Caught on a Houser Helldiver" and released them.

Thanks to Polly Bongard, Adalyn Bennitt and Ollie Hibbler.

MISSOURI
GAME and FISH NEWS

JANUARY 1930 — NUMBER 1 VOLUME 6

The Royal Gorge in Iron County

International Metal Products Company
3110 Park Ave.
St. Louis

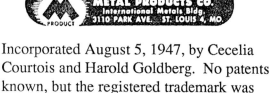

Incorporated August 5, 1947, by Cecelia Courtois and Harold Goldberg. No patents known, but the registered trademark was "Fishsnare". Their product was a fish gripping device, as illustrated in the advertisement from Sports Afield, May, 1948.

Jax Auto Float Company
Kansas City

Made a float which automatically hooked a fish biting the bait. The device was advertised in Outdoor Life, May, 1955.

Judge's Bait Shop
Mt. Vernon

Hand carved experimental lure - 4"

James Eldred Seneker was an attorney, retired Magistrate judge, and avid fisherman. He operated the Judge's Bait Shop in the basement of a rooming house at 221 So. Main. He received Patent No. 2,743,545 on May 1, 1956. The patent also showed a jointed Jaw Breaker, but this model never reached the market. The 2 1/2" Jaw Breaker also was not produced commercially. Judge's Jaw Breaker was the registered trademark. Sales literature described the lure as a "Wig Waggling Wiggler".

The Judge had tried to patent a Lazy Ike type bait earlier, but it was rejected by the Patent Office. He also produced a line of popping bugs for a short time, but found he could not compete with the May Fly Company of Monett.

Bodies for the Jaw Breaker (3 1/2") were made on a machine which a local blacksmith shop made to Seneker's design. Shaping the body involved three separate actions. The Judge could only make about 10 lures per day. His son, Leon, painted most of the lures. Lures were tested in a concrete tank before being sold.

The judge distributed the lures by auto. Most were sold at stores and marinas around Bull Shoals, Table Rock, and Grand Lake of the Cherokees in Oklahoma. The company was in operation between 1956 and 1965. It ceased operation when the Judge suddenly decided the work was interfering with his fishing. Judge Seneker died in 1968 at the age of 87.

Thanks to Douglas, Dwight and Leon Seneker.

Kennard Manufacturing Company
3718 Michigan Ave.
Kansas City

This company was listed in the 1948 Sporting Goods Dealers Directory. They made a Blue Cat Fish Gaff.

Landon Laboratories
117 W. 67th Terrace
Kansas City

Owned by R. C. Wright. Started business in 1955, at 3606 Woodland, in the same building with MarLynn company. Later moved to 67th Terrace. Manufactured and sold a line of

scents called Getzem Fish-bite Bait Lures. It was sold in tubes, with each bait supposedly specific to the fish species given on the label. The company also advertised several items made by The Fisherman's Friend, Fort Branch, Indiana.

Liberty Manufacturing Company
St. Louis

This company was in business from 1956 to 1990. At that time, it was sold and the name changed to Liberty Outdoors, which is in business today. They assembled and sold various items of fishing tackle. The Darting Lizard (3") in the photo, had glass or plastic eyes.

Lipman Lures, Inc.
2528 Dodier Street
St. Louis

Incorporated February 21, 1950, by Harold Lipman, Carl Faur, Denise Derwin, and

Marvin Goldberg. The Lippy's Big Eye lure is marked Pat. Pending. According to Ollie Hibbler, the company also made the Whamee lure, the lower lure in the photo. U. S. trademark 596,288 was registered in June, 1951.

Lur-Ozark Company, Inc.
531 Scarrit Building
Kansas City

Incorporated July 31, 1951, by H. A. Hershfield, Jr., H. P. Giese and Laurence R. Smith. U. S. trademark, BASSANOVA, Serial No. 621,154 was filed November 13, 1951. The address for the trademark was Webb City.

The Marc Reel Company
104 Stoddard Ave.
Dexter

Incorporated February 3, 1947, by Marcus C. McCreary, G. G. Hill, Sr., G. G. Hill, Jr. and Dixie Ruth Hill. McCreary received Patent No. 2,429,637 for the Marc reel on October 28, 1947. Smith (p.145) shows a 1944 advertisement, which gives the B & H Tool and Die Company as the distributor. The company was listed in the 1948 Sporting Goods Dealers Directory.

MarLynn Lure Company
3606 Woodland Avenue
Kansas City
5105 West 40 Highway
Blue Springs

Top: Goldbug   Bottom: Depth Charger

Ted Green and Gale Marcus started the business as a hobby in 1949. They purchased the Naturalure Company from Bert Mayfield in 1953, and began to produce the MarLynn Cobra, a copy of Mayfield's lure. MarLynn Company was incorporated June 16, 1955. That same year, they purchased the Hawk Lure Company from Dave Hawk, Harrisonville, Arkansas, and began making the Goldbug, Thing-A-Ma-Jig and Injured Shad. They began business at the Woodland Avenue address, and later moved to Blue Springs, where they are in business today.

Dave Hawk invented the Texas rig for fishing plastic worms, according to Ted Green. MarLynn was the first to produce the bullet-shaped lead sinker for the Texas rig, but they could only mold a few thousand at a time. An employee of Hornaday adapted one of their bullet molds to rapidly turn out millions of the sinkers, and MarLynn was forced to stop production.

MarLynn also molded the Horsehead Jig for Herter's. This jig eventually became the Roadrunner, made by Blakemore.

Ted Green was Sales Manager for Lutz Pork Bait Company 1962 to 1964. MarLynn bought the Boomerang lure from Lutz in the late 1960s but has not marketed the lure. They continued expansion by purchase of the Houser Fly Company in 1974, but have not marketed any of the Houser products.

Thanks to Ted Green.

Miller Lure Company
P. O. Box 8011
Kansas City

They made a plastic, globe-type lure called Top Kick. It came in two sizes, 3 3/8" and 2 1/2 ".

Missouri Lures Ltd.
32 West 70th Terrace
Kansas City

Emory Henderson, owner. Made a Lucky 66 type lure called Emory's 2 to 1.

Mity Mite Lure Company
Box 103
Lee's Summit

Mity Mite Lure Company started business during 1960s, at 2626 Main Street in Joplin, but later moved to Lee's Summit. It was sold to Gary L. Miller and family in 1977. They incorporated the company June 23, 1977, as Mitey Mite Lure Company, but changed the name to Mity Mite Lure Company September 4, 1977. The incorporation was revoked January 1, 1986. The company made jigs and spinner baits.

Montavy Bait Company
Kansas City

Paul Montavy made a large flyrod popper called the Big Bop in 1954. The popper was one inch in diameter and 1 1/4 inches long. It was marketed by Milford R. Waddell & Associates, 610 E. 47th St., Kansas City.

Mueller-Perry Company
1198 So. Florissant
St. Louis

Incorporated December 21, 1959, by Al W. Mueller, Lyle Perry and E. F. Lammert. The Crazy Legs lure was made in at least four sizes.

Nature Faker Lures, Inc.
Windsor

Wes Allen was the founder of the company in the early 1950s. A man who had worked for Gilmore Tackle Company talked Allen into producing a soft, plastic crawdad. The lure was not successful. Allen then produced soft plastic grasshoppers, crickets, and frogs, with the help of his friend, Jim Wilson, and their families. The company also marketed the Shammy Strip, an artificial pork rind.

Allen received Patent No. 2,712,196 on July 5, 1955, for the No Knot Eyelet, a barbed insert for the end of a flyline. Wes Allen and his friend/attorney, Jim Wilson, formed the Wilson-Allen Corporation to market the eyelet. Allen and Wilson are deceased, but the Corporation is still being operated by the Wilson family.

Wes Allen preferred the inventing end of the business, and left most of the marketing details to the Wilsons. One of his later inventions was the Tip-it Bait Box, a styrofoam box with lids on both ends for removal of worms.

NATURE FAKER
WINDSOR, MISSOURI

No Knot Eyelet
A B C & D LINES

25c PER CARD
Pat. No. 2,712,196
NATURE FAKER INC.
Windsor, Mo.
Directions On Back

Thanks to Mrs. Helen Wilson and Bob Moss.

P & H Bait Company
Palmyra

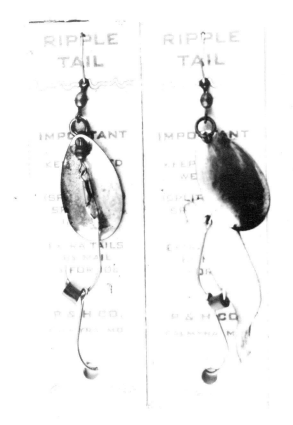

Frank C. Pollard and his wife were caretakers of the Bay de Charles Fishing and Hunting Club, near Palmyra, for 30 years. Even after having a leg amputated at the knee, Pollard fished nearly every day (weather permitting). He began experimenting with lures as early as 1940, and received Patent No. 2,603,024 on July 15, 1952.

The P & H Company, (Pollard and Hoenes), was formed with his son-in-law, Paul Hoenes. They were in business for about 25 years. The registered trademark for the lure was Ripple Tail, (3 inches total length.) Four grandsons helped in the manufacture of the lures. The lures were sold in six or seven states, but apparently were not advertised. They were sold for several years at the concession stand in Bennet Springs State Park.

The Ripple Tail was produced under a royalty arrangement by the Henry Tackle Company of Quincy, Illinois. Years of production are not known.

Thanks to Mrs. Archie Pollard and Mrs. Paul Hoenes.

Paugh Fly Shop
Carthage

Berna Paugh tied flies for the Charles M. Six company. She apparently went into business for herself at one time, possibly after she married Red Hinkle, an Osceola fishing tackle wholesaler.

Phantom Products, Inc.
Kansas City, KS

No. 568,375. It Products, Inc., Kansas City, Kans., now by change of name Phantom Products, Inc., Kansas City, Kans., a corporation of Kansas. Filed Nov. 8, 1948.

For Casting Rods.
Claims use since Sept. 15, 1948.

Produced solid fiberglass fishing rods.

Playmore Products, Inc.
Cape Girardeau

Listed as tackle manufacturer in 8th Fishing Annual (year?).

Reflex Specialties Company
Box 7362,
North Kansas City

The company was incorporated on June 11, 1949, by Paul Prather, Lewis D. Tyhurst, and James G. Tyhurst. Incorporation was revoked January 15, 1960. They made fiberglass rods.

E. T. Senseney
462 Taylor Ave.
St. Louis

Listed in 1948 Sporting Goods Dealers Directory. Sold Dunkit Leader Sinking Paste.

Charles M. Six Company
509 Grant
Carthage

Six Special - 2 1/4"
Skipper - 2 7/8",

Biddlecome-Six Topper Popper

"Ike" Six opened a sporting goods store in Carthage, in 1946. He went into partnership with Cal Biddlecome in 1947. The Biddlecome-Six Company produced bodies for the C. A. Clark Company, and made flies and popping bugs. They began producing the Toppy Popper, but C. A. Clark filed a suit against them because the lure was identical to the Clark Popper Scout. They modified the concave head of the lure by leaving a vertical ridge and continued to produce the Toppy Popper until about 1950, when Six bought-out Biddlecome. Biddlecome then operated on his own for a short time.

The Six Company produced two wooden lures in the early 1950s. The Six Special was marketed locally, but the Skipper was marketed throughout the southeastern states. The company began making jigs and spinner-type baits in the mid 1950s, and these lures became the major products. They were distributed through wholesalers in the southeastern states. The company was purchased by Betts Tackle Company of North Carolina, in about 1978.

Ike Six was made an Honorary Member of the National Fishing Lure Collectors Club in 1992. See the NFLCC Gazette, December, 1992.

Thanks to Ike Six.

B. G. Smith Company
Madison

Bill Smith was a farmer near Madison, when he made The Shark (2 3/4"). The plastic body of the lure was molded for him by a Kansas City firm. Smith assembled the lures and stamped the information on the wings, "Shark Pat Pend. and B G Smith Co Madison MO". About a dozen of the lures were placed on consignment at a local filling station. When Smith tried the lure in a local pond, he decided that they did not have the proper action. "They should have been made of lighter material," he said. When he picked up the lures from the station, one had been sold. The lure was made in the mid 1950s.

Thanks to Kermit Gohring and Bill Smith.

Smith and Yelton Company
Rural Route 5
Kansas City

Hubert R. (Herbie) Smith was a farmer near Cameron, Missouri, when he carved the first Crawpappy lure. He received Design Patent No. Des. 163,973 on July 17, 1951. That same year, the Smith family moved to Kansas City. His brother-in-law, Harry Yelton, persuaded Smith to advertise and sell the Crawpappy. The lure was sold only through magazine ads. Smith handcarved the first lures and they were assembled and painted by the two families. The bodies were carved from mahogany, cherry, and walnut, with the intent of producing lures that would run at different depths. The last 1000 lure bodies were made for Smith on a commercial lathe. These lures were not as effective because the hand carved bodies had a slight hump which the lathe could not duplicate. The antennae were rubber bands.

The lures advertised and sold had a 3"body. A limited number of lures with a 2 3/8" body were produced, but Smith was never satisfied with them. Smith also carved several experimental lures which he did not market.

The Crawpappy lure was a real bass catcher, and Smith was never sure he wanted to share his secret with other fishermen. Consequently, the company was only in business for two or three years. Both Smith and Yelton were carpenters in Kansas City. Harry Yelton was killed in an automobile accident in 1967.

"Herbie" Smith died of a heart attack while on a fishing trip to Truman Reservoir in 1989.

The Craw-Pap shown in the photo is a plastic lure produced by the Rogers Lure Company in recent years. It strongly resembles the Smith and Yelton Crawpappy.

Thanks to Mrs. Hubert Smith, Dale and Harold Yelton.

Stream Sweeper Lures
Mt. Vernon

Leroy Spellman has operated this business from his home since 1948. The name for his company was suggested by Judge Seneker. Spellman and his wife produce a line of jigs, spinner baits, and a road-runner type lure. At one time, he hand-made a limited number of bomber-type lures (1 5/8") for use in white bass fishing.

Strike-it, Inc.
2710 Brannon Avenue
St. Louis

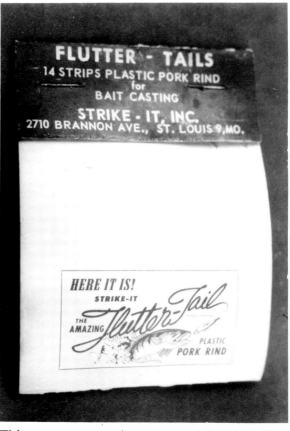

This company was incorporated October 10, 1957, by six men from St. Louis. Leslie J. Haney and Arthur E. McLeod were the major stockholders. The incorporation was revoked January 16, 1961.

Thanks to Frank Warden

Super Products Company
403 Eichelberger
St. Louis

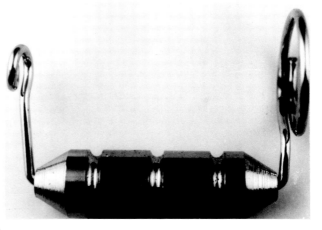

Incorporated June 18, 1956, by Julius C., Francis A. and Margaret I. Engbert. The incorporation was revoked April 7, 1967.

The Turner Company
Hale

Edward Turner operated a garage in La Plata. He moved to Hale in 1946, and was in the hardware business until 1956, when he retired. His son, Delbert, continued the business until 1961. Delbert had the idea for the Spider Lure in about 1949. His idea was to press bait into the springs and when the fish attempted to feed on the bait, it would be snagged by the surrounding hooks.

Ed Turner had a small machine shop and made the lures. He made a jig to twist the wire and stamped out the center disk on a press. Only one batch of about 150 lures was made.

An advertising company in Kansas City was hired to publicize the lur,e but it did not sell well. Only about 100 were sold locally, and through the mail. The Turners started proceedings to patent the lure, but cancelled them because of the lack of interest.

Ed Turner died in 1973. Delbert Turner destroyed the remaining 40-50 lures after he moved to a retirement center where he still resides.

Thanks to Delbert Turner.

The Ward Company
Amsterdam

Virgil Ward owned an appliance store. He is best known as a world champion bass fisherman, but he was also a very successful manufacturer of fishing lures. His first company, Bass Buster Lures, made and sold wooden lures from 1946 through 1950. The lure shown was given to Dan Wyatt by Ward, who said he made it in 1947. The production of wooden lures proved to be costly and unprofitable, so Ward dropped out of the fishing lure business from 1951 to 1955.

The Ward Company began making maribou jigs in 1956. Production increased through the years to include other types of jigs and spinner baits under the Bass Buster label.

Johnson Wax Company bought the business in 1970, and it operated as a division of Johnson Wax under the Bass Buster name. It later became a separate company and continues in business today as Johnson Fishing, Inc.

Thanks to Bill Ward and Jim Stokes.

Tom Ware Fishing Tackle Company
913 Crescent Blvd.
Sedalia

Tom Ware was a contractor who built houses in Sedalia. He came to Sedalia about 1936 from Florida, by way of Louisiana. He was an excellent fly fisherman. The Fly-Plug was produced on a handpress in his basement. At the peak of production, he had two or three people working for him. He received Patent No. 2,913,847 on November 24, 1959.

The lures in the photo are 2" and 1 1/4".

According to friends, he became so involved in the lure company that his contracting business suffered. He moved to Springfield in the 1960s and died there in 1966.

Thanks to Rosemary and Ed Hall.

Wilson-Allen Corporation
Windsor

(See Nature Faker Lure Company)

1964 through 1989

The Postal Service initiated the Zip Code system on July 1, 1963, but it was not really used until early 1964. The Zip Code +4 was initiated twenty years later in 1984. These dates help establish a time period for some companies.

Andrews Lure Company
Lampe

Glen Andrews made a spinner bait called the Stinging Lizard. He was in business for only a couple of years in the mid 60s.

Atomic Bait Company
2607 Heerlein Dr.
St. Joseph

Ted "Sully" Sullwald owner. Thought to have been patented in 1965. "Sully" worked for Swift and Company for 30 years as a mechanic on refrigerated railroad cars. He retired in 1972, and ran Sully's Bait and Tackle Company from 1972 to 1982. He died in 1990.

The bait was produced in a powder form labeled "Golden", and in two hook-ready types labeled "PU" and "Atomic Red". "Sully" had five children, all of whom remember, not-too-fondly, helping to mix the bait in a backyard shed.

The patent was sold in mid 1970s to Dale Liechti, who still runs the Atomic Bait Shop at another location in St. Joseph.

Thanks to Bill Bennitt.

Balsa Baits Company
2251 East Kearney
Springfield

Incorporated March 3, 1975, by Robert L. Martin and Gary P. Twigg. The incorporation was a name change from Westside Tire, Inc. of the same address. The Balsa Boogie in the photo is 2 5/8".

Battlefield Wire Products
Battlefield

James Sparkman started the business in 1972. The company makes blades and wire forms for spinner and buzz baits. Sparkman operated a four-slide machine, which cuts and bends wire. He devised several bends that other people could not make and provided a product which lure manufacturers could not easily mass-produce for themselves. The company currently has 18 full-time employees who turn out over 100,000 wire forms a day. More than 400 lure companies use these forms.

Blakemore Lure Company
North Highway 65
Branson

J. B. Blakemore incorporated the Blakemore Bug Company (7591/2 North Jefferson, Lebanon,) February 9, 1966. The name was changed to Blakemore Lure Company, Branson, on September 12, 1969, with Bert D. Hall, President and Joseph P. Hall, Vice President. The company is currently in business.

Charles Coatney
Gainesville
(Caney Mountain Refuge)

Charlie was an employee of the Department of Conservation and manager of Caney Mountain Refuge. He received no patents and had no trademark. He was well known to fishermen of the Theodosia arm of Bull Shoals Lake. He began commercial production of fishing lures in 1965, and continued until 1975. With the help of his wife and son, he made several types of spinner baits, jigs, and plastic worms, which were sold at local boat docks. The best known was a single spin bait called "Lunker Special".

Thanks to Mrs. Charles Coatney.

Glozier Mfg. Company
1507 Ward Avenue
Caruthersville

Incorporated November 9, 1987, by Thomas C. Hill. The company made a buzz bait called Go Devil.

Ham's Dry Line
Rockaway Beach

Sold fly line dressing in a round cardboard box, according to Bill Calhoun.

Hutchins Tackle
1401 Kingshighway
Independence

Owned by Brent Hutchins. He started business in Independence, but later moved the business to Lincoln. The companies brand name was Assassinator. Crappie jigs were advertised as early as 1974 in Sports Afield. The company was moved to Lincoln, Missouri ,and presently markets jigs, lead heads, and road runner type baits.

K-S Mfg. Company
115 Gum Rd.
Carl Junction

Don Latta
Carthage

Don Latta was an outdoor writer. His column, Me and My Bigmouth, appeared in over 700 newspapers in 26 states. He also was a cartoonist and had a program, Fish Talk, on radio. His book about catching a world record bass, *The $500,0000 Bass*, is a classic.

The lures sold by Don Latta in the 1970s were made by the Ike Six Company. Latta was in business only about two years. His Honey Bee lure had limited distribution.

Incorporated January 30, 1989, by Anthony Sessions and Raymond Knittig. Made plastic novelty lures. The company may have been in business well before 1989, because the lure shown in the photograph was Copyrighted in 1978.

Le-Ber Company
Branson

First company to make 5-1 gears for the early Ambassador reels in the 1960s according to Roger Moore.

Gene Larew Company
Cape Fair-according to Roger Moore
Branson-according to Dan Wyatt

Produced a line of soft plastic lures. Larew was the father of the Electric Blue color, according to Roger Moore, and patented the "Salty Worm" about 1984, according to Dan Wyatt.

Lucky Strike Manufacturing
Box 587
Cassville

This company was controlled by Worm World, Inc., of 704 West Street, Cassville. It was incorporated June 27, 1988, by John and Robyn Hendricks and Mary Allen. It produced plastic worms.

Metro Specialty
4436 St. John
Kansas City

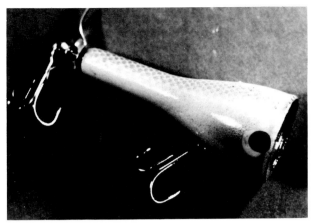

Woodpopper - 3"

Metro Specialty was incorporated February 16, 1973, by James T. Sullivan of Kansas City. Patent No. 3,885,340 was issued to Donald C. Volenec of Omaha, Nebraska, on May 27, 1975. The Glitter Gitter in the photo is 2 1/4". The same lure was sold by Obie Tackle Company, Belleville, Illinois. How confusing!

Ozark Mountain Tackle Company
Carthage

Woodwalker - 3 1/4"

selling the company to Bill Harper in 1989. Luhr Jensen bought the company in 1991.

Thanks to Dan Wyatt.

Woodchopper - 4"

Dan and Phil Wyatt bought the Uncle Asher Lure Company (Arkansas), in 1979, and moved the operation to Carthage as the Ozark Mountain Tackle Company Their first product was the Woodchopper lure. The stainless steel props were the secret of the lures effectiveness. Wyatts developed several more lures before

Semo Tackle Company
Box 443
Sikeston

Produced a double fly similar to the Howard Steen patent.

C. A. Shores
9400 East 69th Terrace
Kansas City

Incorporated January 13, 1965, by Cletus A. Shores, Lewis D. Tyhurst, and James G. Tyhurst. Incorporation was revoked January 15, 1968. The device used a 22 caliber blank cartridge as an alarm. Your line was tied to an arm on top of the box. When a fish jerked the line, the lever released and fired the blank.

Skipper Bait Company
Highway 61 South
Sikeston

Mose Phillips patented the Moss King lure which was made of wood, but I have not found the patent. Johnny Marshall was in charge of manufacturing and sales. The company was in business for only one year, 1965. Lures were sold by mail, as per an advertisement in the June, 1965 issue of Sports Afield. It also was sold at Steinmeyers' Bait Shop at the Duck Creek Wildlife Area, Puxico. The lures in the photo are 2 7/8" (top) and 2 3/8"(bottom).

Thanks to Jim Frazier.

Swamp Fox Lures
429 Saleco Rd.
Sikeston

Albert Roy Marks developed the Moss Boss lure specifically to contend with the thick moss cover at Duck Creek Wildlife Area. The lure resembles the Moss King described above. Marks began experimenting in 1956. His first prototypes were wood, but he also experimented with steel, aluminum, and cork.

He began making the plastic lures (2 3/8" and 2 1/4") from old milk cases, and scraps from a sign company, in 1967. His wife's toaster was used to soften the plastic for molding and all work was done by hand.

There was no need to advertise the Moss Boss. Its success among local fishermen created a demand which far exceeded his primitive production methods. Therefore, he incorporated the Swamp Fox Company in 1973. He had dies made to cast the acrylic bodies for the lures and eliminate the hand labor. He also added a spinner bait and a buzz bait to the line.

The lure business had grown to be more than he really wanted to handle when Marks retired from the grocery business in 1976.

Consequently, he licensed the production, marketing and distribution of the lures to the Stoddard County Community Sheltered Workshop in 1977. His handicapped son had been involved in the Workshop. The Workshop employed 38 handicapped persons, who could turn out 1500 to 2000 Moss Boss Lures per day.

Marketing and distribution soon became more than the Workshop could handle, and in 1979 a deal was made for Heddon to take over those chores. Heddon still markets the Moss Boss.

Thanks to Albert Marks.

Triumph Manufacturing Company
St. Louis

Incorporated December 31, 1964 by Max W. Kramer, Donald B. Kramer and Samuel I. Kohn. The name of the corporation was changed to Mike Machine and Manufacturing Company on October 17, 1968. The incorporation was revoked January 1, 1975. The only product I have seen is a cloth rod bag.

V. J. Lure Company
Marthasville and Wright City

Incorporated August 7, 1987, by Vincent J. Huck, Rayburn E. Rand and Charles W. Purdy. Incorporation was revoked August 25, 1989. They made pork rind strips.

INFORMATION NEEDED

I have little or no information on the following companies. In most cases, the only information is the tackle illustrated or described. Please enlighten me.

Champ-Items, Inc.
St. Louis

Made a plastic funnel which attached to a fruit jar to make a minnow trap. It was called No-Mess Minno Mason.

Cooper Enterprises
Box 515
Neosho

The Little Jul lures in the photo are 3" and 2". A flyrod size (1 3/8") was found on a card stamped L. J. Julius, 145 7th Ave. No., Fort Dodge, Iowa. I assume Julius sold the business to Cooper Enterprises.

Danon Company
Washington

Made a hollow plastic lure into which batteries could be inserted to make lure glow. It was called the Light Emitting Plug (L. E. P.).

Dickson Clawson Company
Kansas City, Kansas

The red cedar tackle box is 8" by 10 1/2" by 18 1/2". It has ten fold-out aluminum trays.

Duble The Katch Tackle Company
804 W. 48th St.
Kansas City

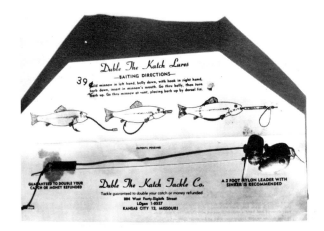

Fishermen's Fly and Tackle Company
Springfield

Fly Boy Lures
4020 State Line Road
Kansas City

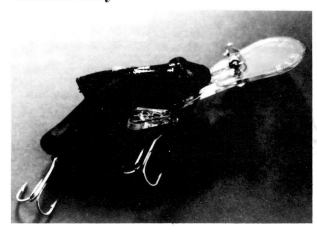

The fins on the side of the Fly Boy (3") may be adjusted to vary the action of the lure.

Henry Fuller
10404 Sheley Road
Independence

Made a lure called Bass Grab. I have seen only a plastic box with the Bass Grab label.

Gourmet Lures, Inc.
Box 7104
Shawnee Mission, Kansas

The lure in the photo is called Captive Catch (1 3/8").

Guy Lure Company
Fenton

The Raider Jr. is only 1/2 inch. I assume they also made a larger lure.

J-D Lures Company
1015 Plymouth Drive
Columbia

Made plastic worms.

J & Jay Bait Company
1243 Cherry St.
Springfield

The Lil Cobra made by this company closely resembled the Little Suzie made by the Ike Six Company.

Johnny's Jig Company
Jefferson City

Made crappie jigs.

Lange Lure Company
Pilot Grove

Made soft plastic critters.

Leslie Lure Company
200 Tall Oaks
Eureka

Made a large Buzz bait called Hawg Squealer.

Midwest Pegboard Company
P. O. Box 1011
Kansas City

Made crappie jigs.

Midwest Sales
Joplin

Made a Lucky 66 type bait called Seminole Sammy.

Newton Mfg. & Sales Company
Box 168
Mission, KS
(Originally in Oklahoma City, Oklahoma)

Norkin Laboratories
809 Wyandotte
Kansas City

The lure in the photo is called The Fluke (1 1/4").

Owensville Sporting Goods, Inc.
208 First St.
Owensville

Made spinner baits and jigs.

Ozark Bait Company
Windsor

The lure in the photo is called Paul's Pal (2 1/4"). A larger, saltwater version also was available. It is made of a rubber-like plastic. The company also made the Red-Fin Minnow shown in the advertisement.

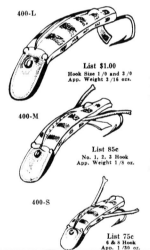

RED - FIN - MINNOW

The all-purpose lure for all fish. For spinning, fly rod casting and trolling. Made of a new latex compound. Will not oxidize. THIS IS NOT A VULCANIZ-ED RUBBER LURE. Soft life-like feel. 99% weedless. Single hook for sport. Play your fish, don't drown him with a mouth full of treble hooks. A deadly killer for large trout and small mouth bass. Comes in three sizes. Twelve color combinations for casting and trolling use weight four to twelve inches from lure.
IMPORTANT: Retrieve and troll very slowly.

OUR SALES POLICY

We do not want slow moving numbers in your stock. Return them. We will replace with numbers of your selection, provided boxes are usable. Otherwise, actual cost of boxes will be made. Do not over buy.

A spoon-type bait coated with the same substance and having a similar skirt was made by the Ozark Bait Company of Shelbyville, Indiana. Both of these lures were found in remainders from the Berry-Lebeck factory. They were produced prior to 1951, when Berry-Lebeck ceased operations.

Ozark Bait Company
4218 Hearnes Boulevard
Joplin

Incorporated December 15, 1969, by John R. Smith. Incorporation was revoked July 12, 1971.

Piney River Bass Flies
Address unknown

Presto Knocker Company
Carthage

R. B. S. Lure Company
Box 20112
St. Louis

The lure in the photo is called Van De Reit's Super Spoon (2").

Spurgeon Lures
Eminence

This company was owned by Orville E. Spurgeon. The lure is called the Crooked Hooker (3 1/4").

E. S. Stofer Manufacturing Company
322 Shukter Boulevard
Kansas City

Warren Platt has a 9 foot, Calcutta bamboo rod made by this company. The rod has brass fittings and a nickel plated reel seat.

Stoner Machine and
Manufacturing Company
St. Louis

This company's Lucky Twister (2 1/4") strongly resembles the Twirl-a-Lure made by tool and die workers at Carter Carburetor Company.

Structure Lure Company
Galena

Made jigs.

Three J Bait Company
Box 140
Brookline

Made a spinner bait called Motor Mouse.

Thulco Products
174 West Kirkham Rd.
St. Louis

Ultra Lure
Box 2058
Springfield

Made spinner baits called Explorer and
Fascinator.

Art Varner Fly Company
Salem

This company apparently produced flies and
plastic worms. They also sold fly fishing
equipment.

Wally R. Lure Company
Box 2421
Overland

The lure in the photo is called Sting Ray
(2 1/4").

Willey-J-Bait Company
211 North Market
Springfield

Made a spinner bait called Fuzz Bug.

K. C. Zumwalt Company
1810 Joplin St.
Joplin

HOMEMADE

These lures were hand carved or made in home workshops in limited quantities. They usually were sold from the home or in local stores.

Enoch A. "Buck" Buchanan
Perryville

Buck was a Conservation Agent with the Department of Conservation. His lures were given or sold mainly to other Department employees. The three hooker is 3 1/4" and the two hooker is 3".

Carter Carburetor
St. Louis

Tool and Die makers at Carter made a die to stamp out the lure they called Twirl-A-Lure (1 1/2"). They made the copper lures for themselves and gave some to other fishermen. The die and the lure bodies were made when the boss was out to lunch. The Lucky Twister made by the Stoner Machine and Manufacturing Company seems to be an off-shoot of this lure.

The workers also made a die for cutting willow leaf spinners. They cut the spinners from the bottom panel of aluminum storm doors.

Thanks to Steve White.

Bill Debo
Devil's Elbow

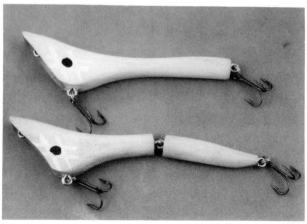

Bill Debo is one of the Debos of Devil's Elbow, woodworkers since 1830, according to their business card. He currently makes hand carved lures for sale at local stores and at craft shows. The crossed lines around the eye of his Debo Demon (3" and 4") are his mark.

Rube Dick
Golden

Top Left: Smith Bros. - 2 7/8"
Bottom Left: Ernie Enfield - 3 1/2"
Top Right: Rube Dick - 3 1/8"
Bottom Right: Unknown Springfield - 3 1/8"

Rube Dick was a part-time farmer and guide on the White and Kings rivers from 1930 to 1960. He lived near the Arkansas line, between the two rivers. Dick whittled and sold the Ozark Ike in the 1950s. The lure in the photo was received from John Hubbard, Stockton, a friend of Dick.

J. D. Fletcher, Devil's Den Resort, bought Dick's guide boats in 1959. He remembers Dick as a rough, tough Ozarkian. Dick died in 1979.

Eaton
Granby

Mr. Eaton reportedly was a barber in Granby. Lures are of two types: wooden bodied lures with a diving lip which incorporates a steel ball bearing (2-2 1/2") and metal lures (stainless steel or monel metal - 1 1/2"-2") which also incorporates the ball bearing. Some of the lures are stamped "Eaton" or "Janie".

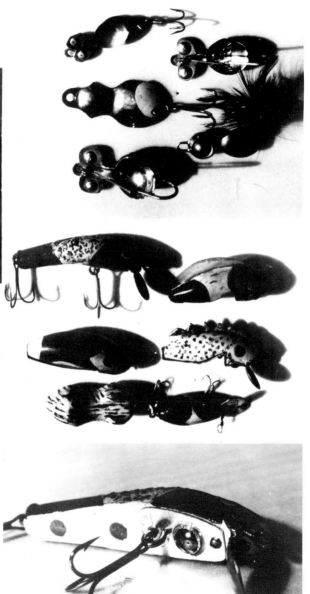

Thanks to Roger Yount.

Ernie Enfield
Golden

Ernie Enfield was born in St. Joseph, and raised in Kansas City. He moved to Golden in 1939. Fishing and whittling were his major pastimes. He began whittling the Ozark Ike type lures in 1955. The demand in later years forced him to begin cutting the outline of lures with a jig saw before carving them to final shape. The success of the lures is described in an article in the April, 1974 issue of Sports Afield. His largest order was for 1,400 lures from a float trip operator, probably J. D. Fletcher, Devil's Dive Resort. Enfield made the lures until at least 1970. See Rube Dick for an illustration of the lure.

Ted Eudy
Piedmont

H. Fritschen
8729 Granada
Jennings

This unique weedless hook (1") was made using the hinge from eyeglasses. The box, (postmarked 1947), is addressed to the Berry-Lebeck Company. Apparently, the inventor wanted to interest Berry-Lebeck in making the product.

Earl Lutes
Lutesville

Ted Eudy was an employee of the Forestry Division of the Missouri Department of Conservation. He had no patents or trademarks. The lures were turned on a lathe in his garage during the 1970s. The topwater lure is 2 3/8" and the underwater is 3 1/2 ". His production was very limited and sold locally. Most of his sales seem to have been to other Department employees. Ted died in 1989.

Earl Lutes was employed in the Forestry Division of the Department of Conservation. His lures (4 1/4") were given or sold mainly to other employees.

Shallow Water Bait Company
309 Hereford
Branson

Top: Frog - 3"
Bottom: Varmint -2 1/2"

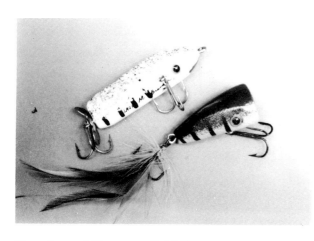

Top: Lazy Minnow - 2 1/2"
Bottom: Blooper - 1 3/4"

These lures are hand carved and painted by Albert Ford. His father, Mitch, was a guide in the Branson area for 30 years and worked for Jim Owens for 20 years. Albert started making the Blooper lure in 1967. He added other lures to the line during the years, and currently sells his lures through local businesses in Branson. The Frog has deer skin legs and the Varmint has hair from the tail of a horse. I also have seen lures dated 1984, and labeled Albert Ford, Kansas City.

Show-me Wooden Classics
517 Lemonwood
St. Louis

Nick Hamra was a guide on several Missouri lakes. He began making the Nick's Zip Stick (4 1/4") in 1985. Hamra also produced a limited number of individualized presentation lures for the Missouri Conservation Federation.

Smith Brothers
White River Region

Dudley Murphy, from whom I obtained the lure, said that the Smith Brothers were old time guides on the White River, and carved the lures while guiding float trips. The lure is very similar to the Ozark Ike made by Rube Dick and Ernie Enfield. See Rube Dick for picture.

Woodchip and Sawdust Shop
Farmington

Robert H. Gaines is a woodworker who makes lures as gifts for his friends and sells a few at meetings of woodworkers. In addition to the two lures (4 1/2") illustrated, he makes a series of gag lures and oversized reproductions of commercially produced lures.

Unknown
Springfield

No information except lures illustrated. The Ozark Ike type lure is nearly identical with the lures of Rube Dick and Ernie Enfield. See Rube Dick for picture.

Unknown
Kansas City

These two lures (3" and 3 1/4") were found in the Kansas City area by Jack Looney. They have several of the characteristics of the patent issued on June 4, 1918, to W. H. Shuff, Kansas City.

Unknown
St. Louis

These two lures (3") were made in the St. Louis area, according to Jim Muma. The spoon is brass and the raised bodies seem to be made of auto body putty.

William G. Wade
Savannah

Mr. Wade taught in the Fillmore school district from 1924 to 1930 and was head of the agriculture department at Savannah R-3 from 1930 to 1965.

While he was on a fishing trip to Minnesota, his fishing companion lost a favorite lure, the Osaca Minnow. Wade made a copy of the lure in his woodworking shop. The copy proved to be effective and Wade made many more. He also reproduced several of the more popular lures of major manufacturers, such as the Heddon 210 and the Bass Oreno. His workshop contained hundreds of these reproductions at the time of his death in November, 1992, at the age of 93.

Thanks to Ron Wade and Bill Bennitt.

COMPANIES IN BUSINESS-1992

The following companies were listed in the 1992 American Business Directory or can be found on retailer's shelves.

Able 2 Products
504 East 13th St.
Cassville

Alexander's Angling Products
3521 Power Dr.
Kansas City

Alron Lures
702 S. Main
Clinton

Bass Napper Manufacturing
2201 West Battlefield
Springfield

Bee Jay Bait Company
North Kansas City

Blakemore Lure Company
North Highway 65
Branson
Registered trademark is Road Runner.

Early Bird Baits
Route 5, Box 324
Reed Springs

Gray's Lazy Hooker
Route 2, Box 187
Warsaw

Hawg-Jaw Tackle and Supply
Box 121
Cape Fair

Heluva Lure Corporation
702 Price
Versailles

Jewel Industries
Highway 101
Bakersfield

Johnson Fishing, Inc.
301 Main Street
Amsterdam

Laker
Camdenton

Liberty Outdoors, Inc.
500 Bittner Street
St. Louis

Lucky Strike Manufacturing
704 West Street
Cassville

MarLynn Lure Company
5105 West US 40
Blue Springs

Moore Fishing Enterprises Inc.
Box 8656
Independence

Prairie Hollow Tackle Company
903 Kingscross Road
Blue Springs

Noel A Price Company
200 West 80th Terrace
Kansas City

Rainbow Lures
299 East Commercial Street
Springfield

Ray-Lee Tackle
Independence

Rieadco Corporation
605 North High Street
Independence

Jim Rogers Lures
928 East 12th Street
Lamar

Shiloh Lure Company
103 East 4th Street
Appleton City

Soft Pak U S A
North Highway 65
Branson

Strike Zone Lures
Box 273
Clinton

Tee Cee Tackle
Box 30
Bradleyville

Wilson-Allen Corporation
106 North Main Street
Windsor

Young Manufacturing Company
North Busch
Mountain Grove

EARLY WHOLESALERS AND DISTRIBUTORS

Missouri was not blessed with any of the major manufacturers of fishing tackle but the state did have some major distributors of early tackle, especially in Kansas City and St. Louis.

Butler Brothers
St. Louis

Distributed a general line of fishing tackle made by major manufacturers. A 1919 catalog indicated the company was in business during the early 1900s.

R. S. Elliot Arms Company
Kansas City

Distributed fishing tackle of major manufacturers. Years of operation unknown.

Gateway Sporting Goods Company
1330 Main Street
Kansas City

Began operations in 1918. Date of closing unknown, but known to have been in business during 1960s. Sold tackle labeled with the name of the manufacturer but also sold tackle made for them and labeled with their house brand, Gateway. Were a major distributor for C. A. Clark and Berry-Lebeck.

Leacock Sporting Goods Company
921 Locust St.
St. Louis

Started in business in 1921. Sold a general line of sporting goods. Tackle was made for them by other companies and labeled Leacock. In later years, apparently specialized in fly fishing equipment. Trademark 426,480 registered December 24, 1946. A letter on Leacock company letterhead was signed by Glenn A. Beede in April, 1949.

Lotz Brothers
147 North Main
St. Louis

They advertised a fish lure (bait?) in 1914. Reported to have sold a general line of fishing tackle. Years of operation unknown.

McClean's Sporting Goods
400 South 7th
St. Louis

Company was listed in 1948 Sporting Goods Dealers Directory.

Rawlings Sporting Goods
620 Locust Street
St. Louis

Sold general line of fishing tackle. A copy of their 1901 catalog (No.11), indicates they were in business prior to 1900.

Richards and Conover Hardware Company
Kansas City

Their 1939 catalog lists a general line of fishing tackle labeled with the manufacturer's name.

Schmelzer Arms Company
700 Main Street
Kansas City

Their 1898 catalog is designated as Catalog 783, which indicates they were in business well before 1900. Sold a general line of fishing tackle with the manufacturer's name, but also had tackle made for them and labeled Schmelzer. Luckey (p.407) discusses a bait called Spike Tail Motion Bait sold by Schmelzer.

Shapleigh Hardware Company
St. Louis

Rogers Brothers Hardware Company of Philadelphia sent August Frederick Shapleigh to open a St. Louis branch in 1843. The store was located at 414 Main Street and was called Rogers, Shapleigh Company. The company name was changed to Shapleigh, Day and Company in 1847 when Rogers died. This company put out its first catalogue in 1853. Day retired in 1863 and the company existed as A. F. Shapleigh until 1880, when it was incorporated as A. F. Shapleigh and Cantwell Hardware Company. The name of A. F. Shapleigh and Company was restored after the retirement of Cantwell in 1886. Fire destroyed the business in 1886, but it was quickly rebuilt at 519-521 North Main Street and North Vine.

A. F. Shapleigh retired in 1900 and died in 1902 at the age of 92. The company was reorganized as Norvell-Shapleigh Hardware Company in 1901. It carried this name until 1918 when it became Shapleigh Hardware Company, the name it carried until its closing in 1959.

Simmons Hardware Company
St. Louis

Edward Campbell Simmons was a junior partner in the hardware firm of Wilson, Levering and Waters when Levering died in 1862. The name then became Waters, Simmons and Company which was changed to E. C. Simmons and Company in 1872 with the retirement of Waters. Simmons Hardware Company was incorporated in 1874. The company was located at Ninth and Spruce Street with warehouses between Seventh and Eighth Streets on Poplar. Simmons apparently had a manufacturing branch because products with the Simmons brand name were labeled "manufacturers and distributors." Shapleigh Hardware purchased Simmons in 1940.

Walton Supply Company
3507 Juniata Street
St. Louis

This advertisement appeared in the Hunting and Fishing Magazine for July, 1938, and said, "Write for catalog of fish traps, fish lures, keep-alive bait hooks and other specialties for fishermen."

Witte Hardware Company
St. Louis

Sold general line of fishing tackle under manufacturer's name. Years of operation unknown.

Wyeth Company
St. Joseph

Began in 1859. A 1962 catalog indicates they were in business at that time. Sold a general line of fishing tackle with no house brand.

PATENTS ISSUED TO MISSOURIANS

Patents issued to Missourians could be determined in the Index of Patents issued from the United States Patent Office prior to 1954. The format of the Index was changed in 1954. The new format made it impossible to trace the origin of a patent unless you knew the patent number or the patentee's name and year patent was issued.

St. Louis

W. H. GREGG.

ARTIFICIAL WORM-BAIT FOR FISHING.

No. 185,914.   Patented Jan. 2, 1877.

FIG.1.

ATTEST: INVENTOR:

Robt Burns   William H. Gregg
H. Hutchins   By Knight Bro.
                                Attys.

F. DE FOREST. Desoto

FISH HOOK.

No. 264,256.   Patented Sept. 12, 1882.

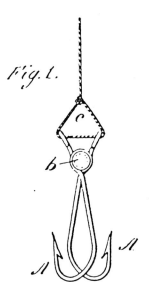

Fig. 1.

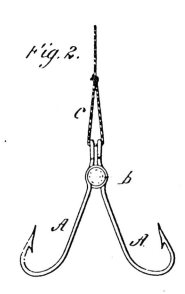

Fig. 2.

WITNESSES:

Dinn Twitchell

C. Sedgwick

INVENTOR:

F. De Forest

BY   Munn & Co

ATTORNEYS.

C. HYMERS.   St. Louis

SELF ADJUSTING FISH-SHAPED FISH HOOK HOLDER.

No. 273,996.   Patented Mar. 13, 1883.

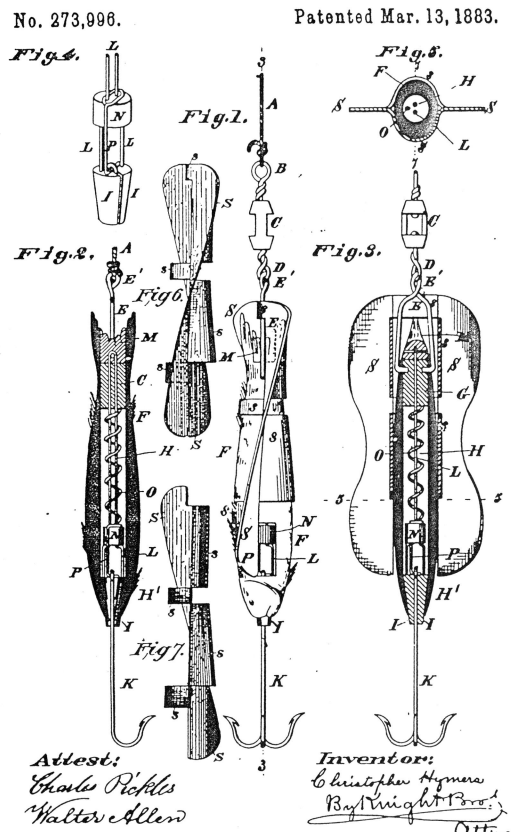

Attest:
Charles Pickles
Walter Allen

Inventor:
Christopher Hymers
By Knight Bros.
Attys

Nevada

No. 666,398.

W. H. TALBOT.
FISHING REEL.
(Application filed July 28, 1900.)

Patented Jan. 22, 1901.

(No Model.)

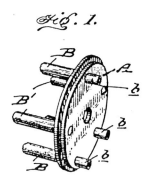

Fig. 1.

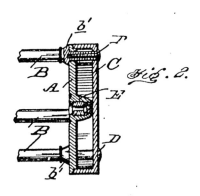

Fig. 2.

Inventor

William H. Talbot,

By Jos. H. Hunter

Attorney,

Witnesses:

58

H. A. WILLIAMSON.   St. Louis
ANIMATED MINNOW.
APPLICATION FILED APR. 4, 1910.

866,068.   Patented Aug. 2, 1910.

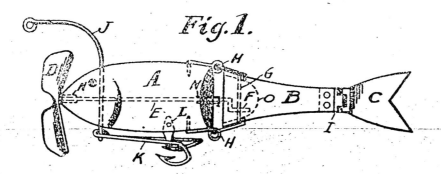

Fig.1.

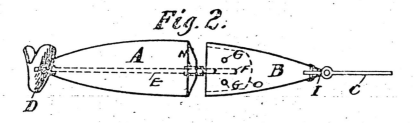

Fig.2.

Fig.3.

59

F. W. BREDER & J. H. LOYD.   Springfield
ARTIFICIAL BAIT.
APPLICATION FILED APR. 19, 1909.

972,748.   Patented Oct. 11, 1910.

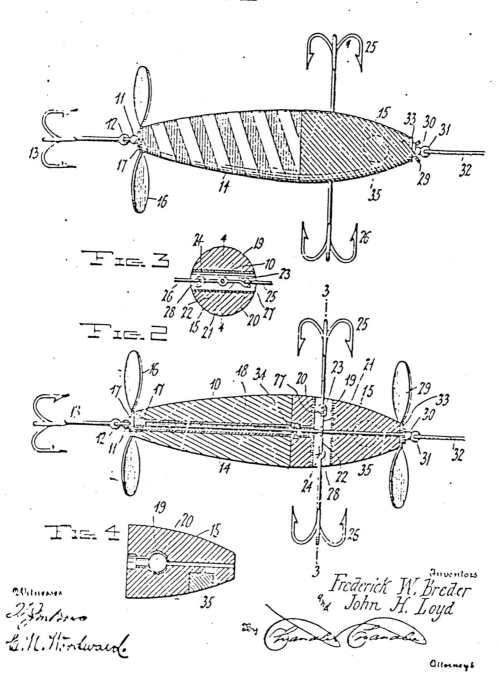

Fig. 1

Fig. 3

Fig. 2

Fig. 4

Inventors
Frederick W. Breder
and John H. Loyd
By

Attorneys

J. H. FULLER & A. MILLER.   Moberly

FISHING DEVICE.

APPLICATION FILED AUG. 15, 1911.

1,038,866.   Patented Sept. 17, 1912.

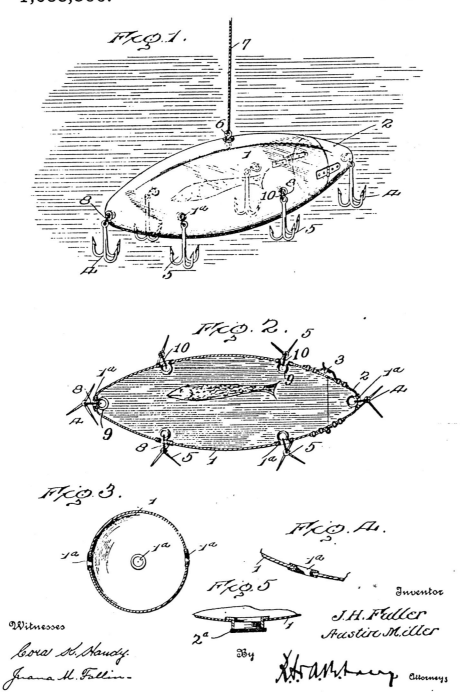

FIG. 1.

FIG. 2.

FIG. 3.

FIG. 4.

FIG. 5.

Witnesses

Cora L. Handy.

Juana M. Fallin.

Inventor

J. H. Fuller

Austin Miller

By

Attorneys

1.072.672. COMBINED FISH-HOOK AND ANIMAL-
TRAP. WELCOME F. SWEET, St. Louis, Mo., assignor
to Eddleman's Never Fail Fish Hook and Animal Trap
Company, Mineral Wells, Tex., a Corporation of Texas.
Filed Nov. 4, 1912. Serial No. 729,419. (Cl. 43—31.)

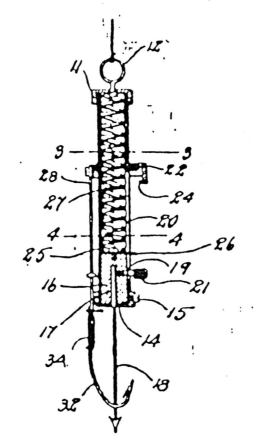

The combination with a tubular body having a spring
pressed spear carrying block and a latch for holding said
block retracted, of a rod connected to said latch the
forward end of which rod projects beyond the end of
the tubular body and is bent to form a loop and a hook,
said loop and hook being spaced apart, a fish hook having
its shank inclosed by the loop on the rod with the eye
of said fish hook engaged by the hook on the rod, and a
fastening means encircling the shank of the fish hook
and the parts of the rod between the loop and the
hook.

C. WILT.   Springfield
MINNOW.
APPLICATION FILED AUG. 26, 1911.   RENEWED FEB. 6, 1913.

1,073,199.   Patented Sept. 16, 1913.

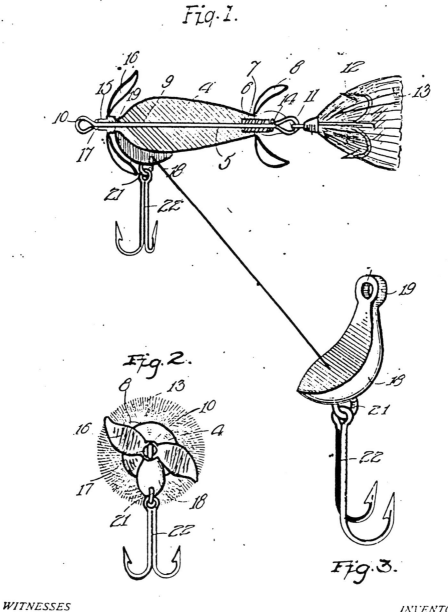

Fig. 1.

Fig. 2.

Fig. 3.

WITNESSES

INVENTOR

Clinton Wilt

By E. E. Trueman, Attorney

A. SAMPEY.
ARTIFICIAL ELECTRIC MINNOW.
APPLICATION FILED NOV. 9, 1914.

1,159,278.

Patented Nov. 2, 1915.

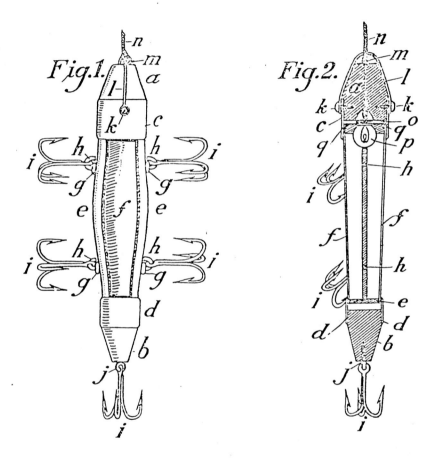

Fig.1.

Fig.2.

WITNESSES:

Perry T. Allen
B. W. Lamb

Alfred Sampey

INVENTOR

1,184,588. Patented May 23, 1916.

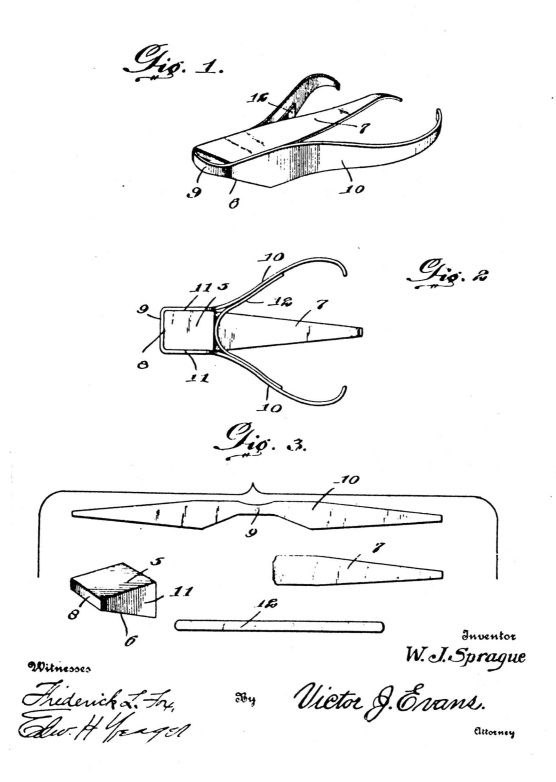

Fig. 1.

Fig. 2.

Fig. 3.

Witnesses
Frederick L. Fox,
Edw. H Yeager

Inventor
W. J. Sprague

By Victor J. Evans.
Attorney

S. ARNOLD. Kansas City

CASTING WEIGHT FOR FISHING LINES.

APPLICATION FILED OCT. 7, 1916.

1,232,167.

Patented July 3, 1917.

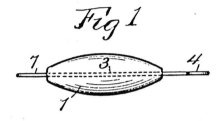

Fig 1

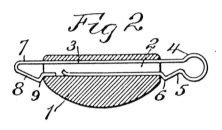

Fig 2

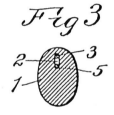

Fig 3

WITNESS:
R.E. Hamilton

INVENTOR.
Sigel Arnold
BY Warren D. House
His ATTORNEY

Kansas City

W. H. SHUFF.

ARTIFICIAL BAIT KNOWN AS PLUGS OR WOOD MINNOWS.

APPLICATION FILED JULY 19, 1917.

1,268,635.

Patented June 4, 1918.

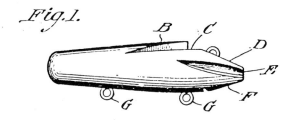

Fig. 1.

Fig. 2.

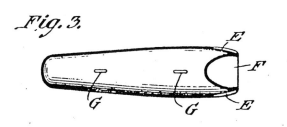

Fig. 3.

Inventor

William H. Shuff

Witness

S. ARNOLD.
ARTIFICIAL FISH BAIT.
APPLICATION FILED SEPT. 27, 1917.

1,272,183.

Patented July 9, 1918.

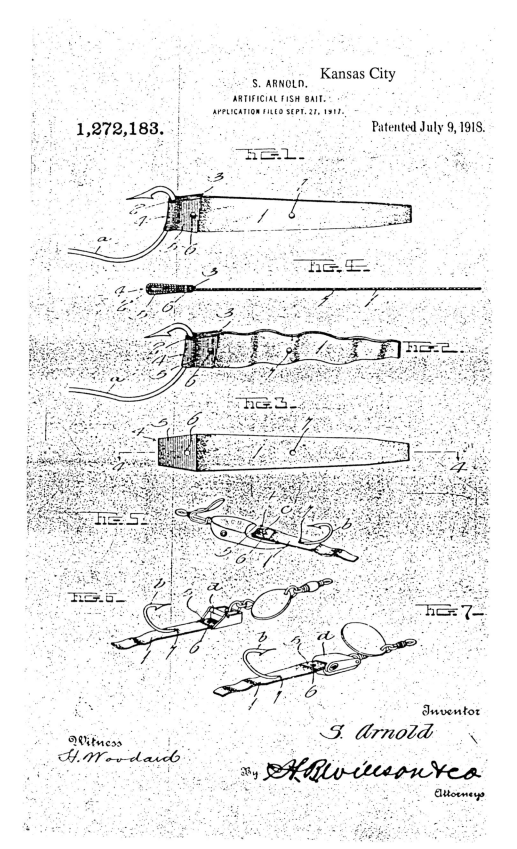

Inventor
S. Arnold

Witness
H. Woodard

By H. R. Wilson & Co
Attorneys

W. C. TAYLOR

ARTIFICIAL BAIT FOR FISH

Filed June 9, 1922

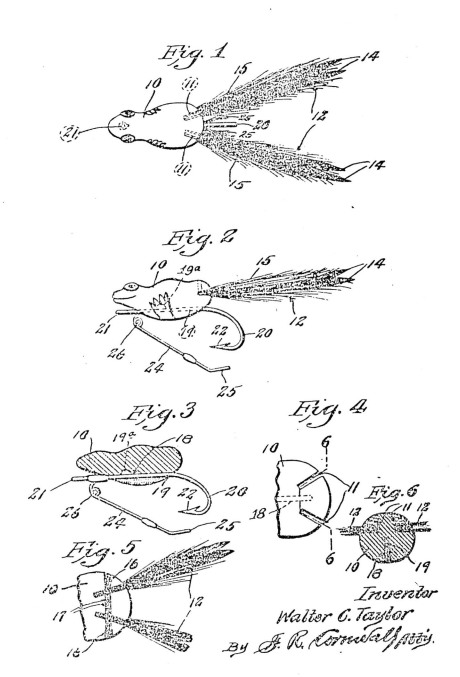

Fig. 1

Fig. 2

Fig. 3   *Fig. 4*   *Fig. 6*

Fig. 5

Inventor
Walter C. Taylor
By J. R. Cornwall, atty.

G. W. LUCAS. Kansas City
FISHHOOK FISHING MACHINE.
APPLICATION FILED MAR. 7, 1921.

1,383,474.

Patented July 5, 1921.
2 SHEETS—SHEET 1.

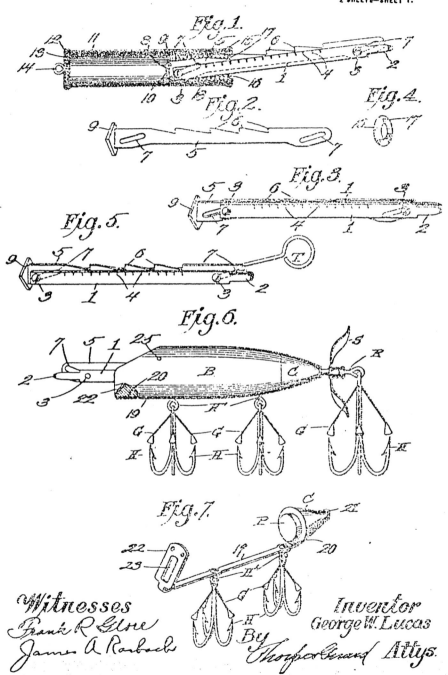

Fig.1.

Fig.2.

Fig.4.

Fig.3.

Fig.5.

Fig.6.

Fig.7.

Witnesses
Frank R Gilroe
James A Rachbach

Inventor
George W. Lucas
By
Thorpe & Grant Attys.

Kansas City

G. W. LUCAS.

FISHHOOK FISHING MACHINE.

APPLICATION FILED MAR. 7, 1921.

1,383,474. **Patented July 5, 1921.**

2 SHEETS—SHEET 2.

Fig. 8.

Fig. 10

Fig. 9.

Witnesses
Frank R Glove
James A Rarbach

Inventor
George W. Lucas
By Thorpe & Gerard Attys.

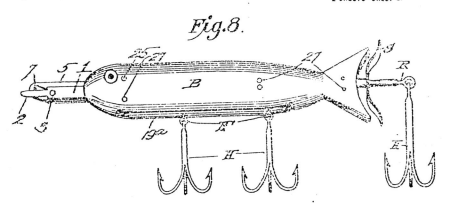

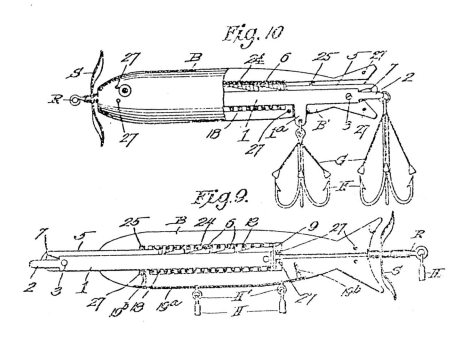

Dec. 18, 1928.

St. Louis

P. J. BODE

FISHING TACKLE

Filed Oct. 5, 1927

1,696,026

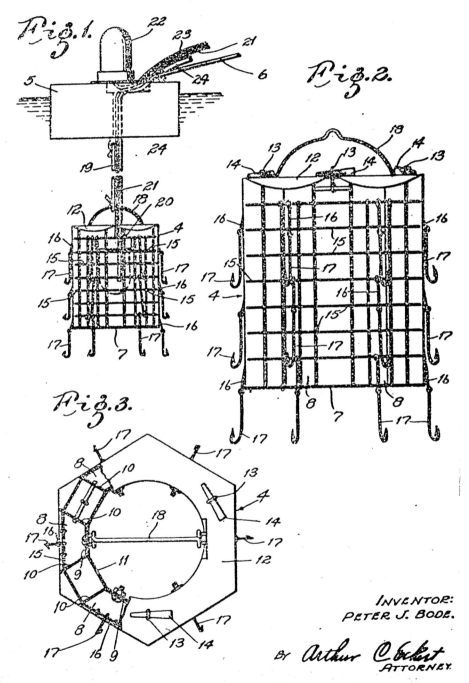

Fig.1.

Fig.2.

Fig.3.

INVENTOR:
PETER J. BODE.

By Arthur C. Eckert
ATTORNEY.

Patented Mar. 3, 1931

1,795,238

UNITED STATES PATENT OFFICE

DELLAS J. SPENCE, OF BRANSON, MISSOURI

FISH BAIT

No Drawing.   Application filed May 19, 1928.   Serial No. 279,203.

My invention relates to improvements in bait and primarily to fish bait,—although the same is capable of use for baiting traps to attract certain animals, such as opossum and skunk.

An important object of the invention is to provide a fish bait which will have the requisite decomposed odor to attract cat fish and other sucker mouthed fish, carp, buffalo, red horse, etc.—and in short the vast majority of the species of inland fish,—and which bait will have a body of such consistency as to enable it to be made up into individual baits and sold in cans or boxes.

A further object of the invention is to provide a bait, as characterized, which will readily hold its form and which will not readily decompose in use.

A further object of the invention is to provide a solid fish bait having decomposed or fermented odor and which includes novel means and compositions of elements for accentuating said decomposed odor and for giving the bait a further characteristic of sweetness, which is attractive to practically all kinds of fish and particularly to the species hereinabove mentioned.

In carrying out the invention I prefer to use the following ingredients in substantially the proportions set forth:

Solids.

Whole wheat flour	1 bushel
Cornmeal	½ peck
Cheese	1 bushel

Liquids

Corn syrup	1 quart
Sorghum syrup	1 quart
Licorice, 1 large commercial stick dissolved in water	½ pint
Coffee and chicory solution	1 quart
Yeast cake dissolved in water	½ pint
Cotton seed oil	3 pints

The proportions of the ingredients may be otherwise given as follows:

Solids

	Per cent
Whole wheat flour	50
Corn flour	10
Cheese	40
Total	100

Liquids

	Per cent
Corn syrup	20
Sorghum syrup	20
Licorice (dissolved in water)	5
Coffee and chicory solution	20
Yeast (dissolved in water)	5
Cotton seed oil	30
Total	100

In compounding the bait the wheat flour, corn flour and cheese are ground up and thoroughly mixed in a bowl. The liquids in the proportions mentioned are separately mixed and thoroughly stirred in another vessel. Then the entire quantity of the liquid is poured into the mass of wheat flour, corn flour and cheese to reduce the latter mixture to a paste having about the consistency of dough.

The paste, thus formed, is made into pellets of desired size and packed in an air-tight box ready for use.

The wheat flour contains or supplies the adhesive properties necessary to hold the pellet together so that it will stay on the hook. The corn flour gives the bait a flavor and bulk. The flavor given by the corn flour in combination with the other ingredients is that of fermentation and this characteristic makes the bait particularly attractive to sucker mouth fish, such as carp and buffalo.

The cheese is used as a body along with the corn flour and wheat flour and is employed

Fig.1.

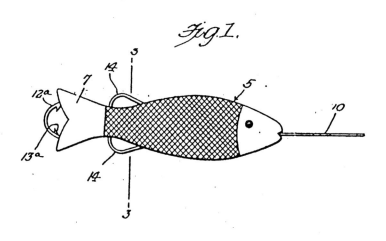

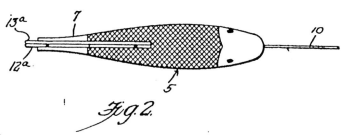

Fig.2.

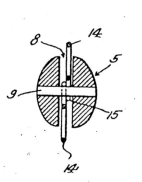

Fig.3.

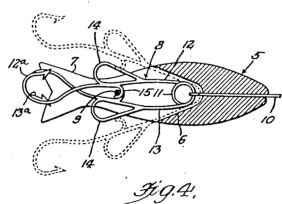

Fig.4.

Inventor
Herman G. Swearingen,

By *Clarence A. O'Brien*
Attorney

April 19, 1932.

Trenton

W. A. HERINGTON

1,854,696

FISH LURE

Filed May 21, 1931

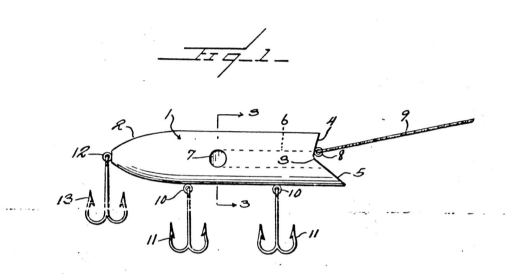

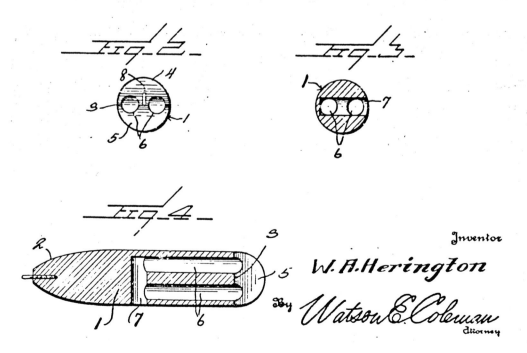

Inventor

W. A. Herington

By Watson E. Coleman

Attorney

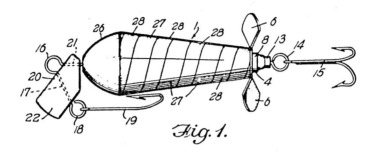

Fig. 1.

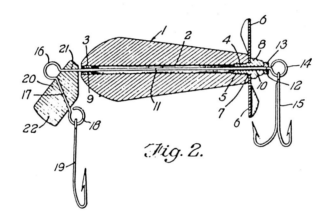

Fig. 2.

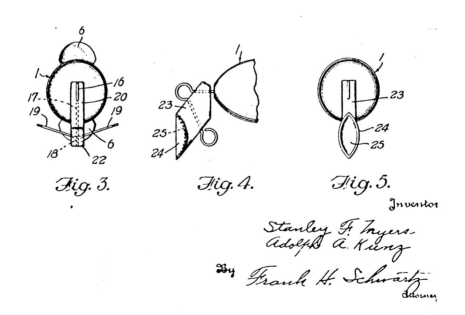

Fig. 3.   *Fig. 4.*   *Fig. 5.*

Inventor
Stanley F Myers
Adolph A. Kunz
By Frank H. Schwartz
Attorney

Oct. 9, 1934.

Kansas City

J. R. PLASTERS

1,975,864

FISH STRINGER

Filed April 16, 1932

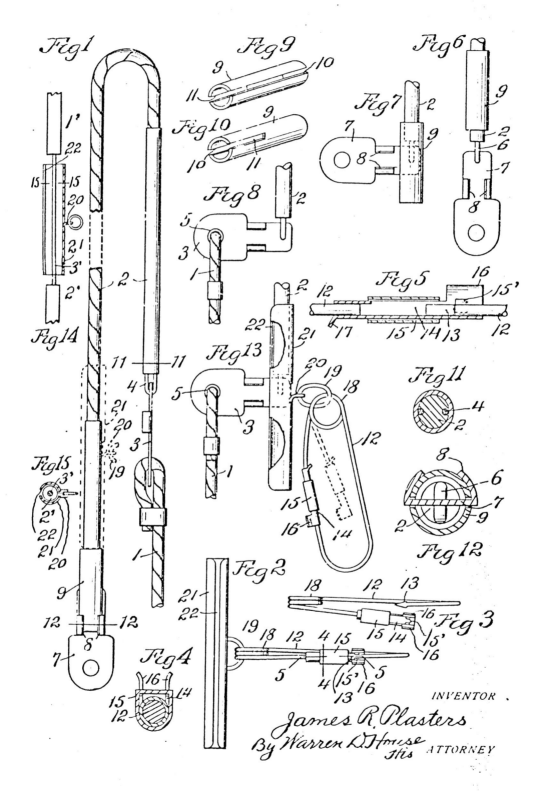

INVENTOR

James R. Plasters

By Warren D. House His ATTORNEY

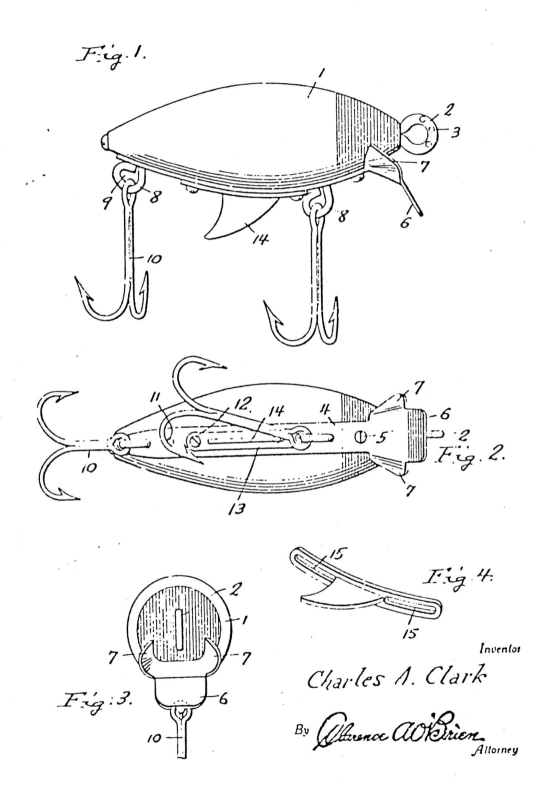

Fig. 1.

Fig. 2.

Fig. 3.

Fig. 4.

Inventor

Charles A. Clark

By Clarence A. O'Brien

Attorney

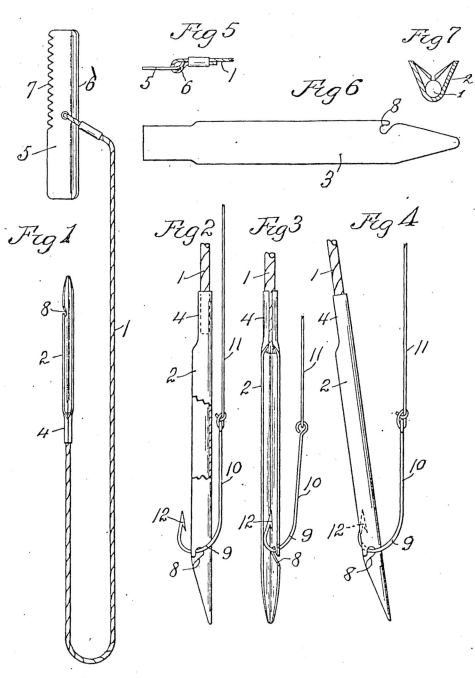

INVENTOR
James R. Plasters
BY
Warren D. House
His ATTORNEY

Feb. 26, 1935.   C. D. McDOWELL   1,992,874

ILLUMINATED BOB FOR FISHLINES

Filed May 11, 1934   2 Sheets—Sheet 1

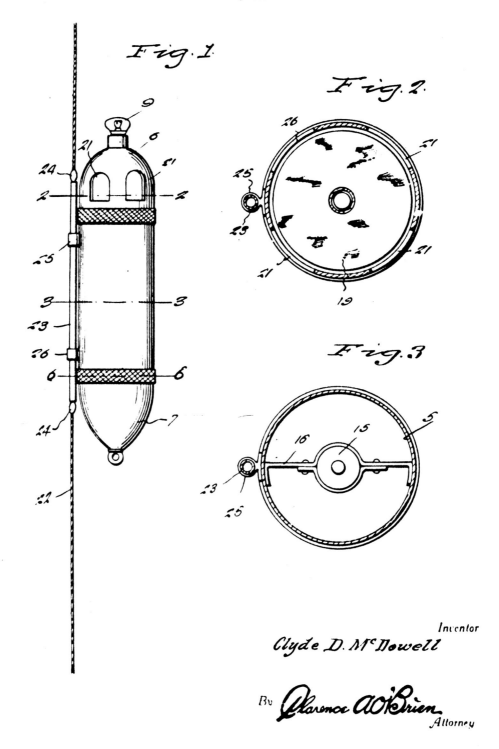

Fig. 1

Fig. 2

Fig. 3

Inventor

Clyde D. McDowell

By *Clarence A. O'Brien*

Attorney

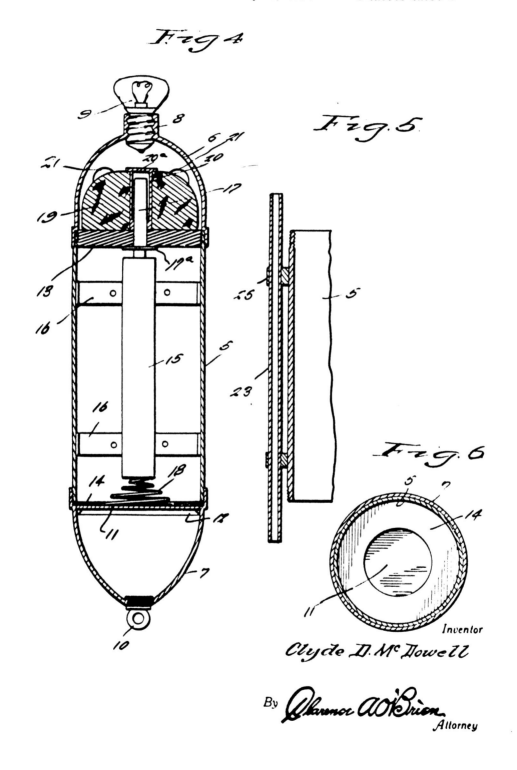

Fig 4

Fig. 5

Fig. 6

Inventor

Clyde D. McDowell

By Clarence A. O'Brien
Attorney

81

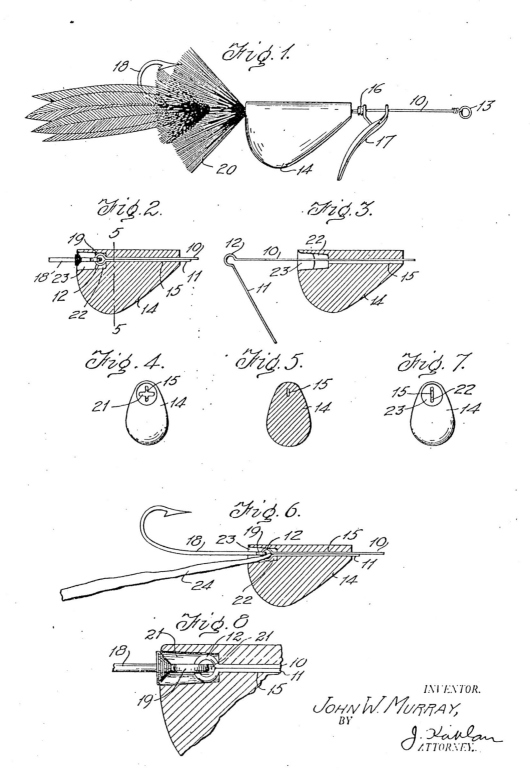

INVENTOR.

JOHN W. MURRAY,
BY

J. Kaplan
ATTORNEY.

March 30, 1943.

M. M. FENLEY

2,315,322

FISHING FLOAT

Filed Nov. 4, 1941

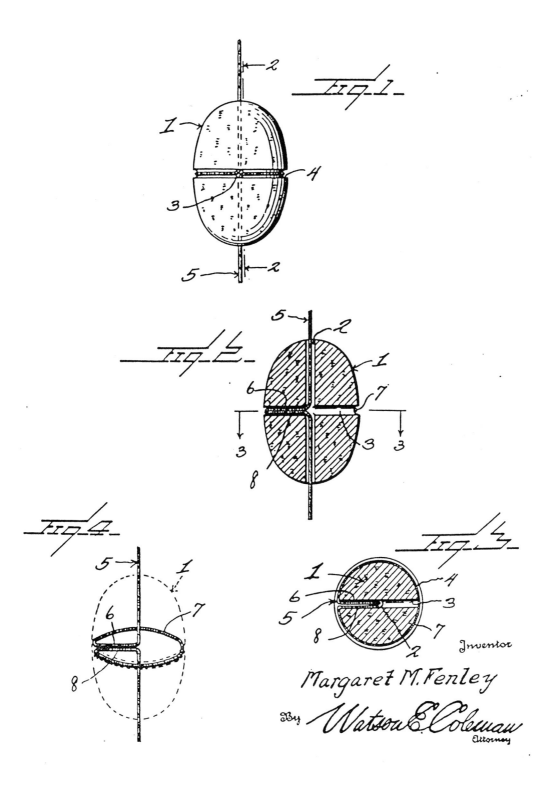

Fig.1

Fig.2

Fig.4

Fig.3

Inventor

Margaret M. Fenley

By Watson E. Coleman

Attorney

Dexter

Oct. 28, 1947.

M. McCREARY

2,429,637

FISHLINE REEL

Filed Oct. 18, 1945

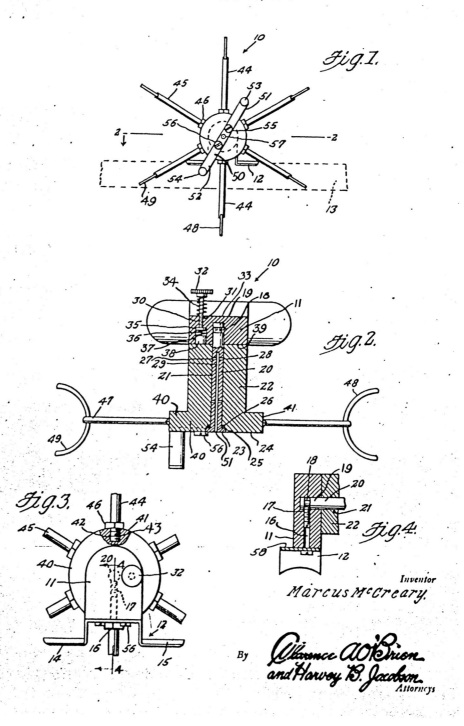

Fig. 1.

Fig. 2.

Fig. 3.

Fig. 4.

Inventor

Marcus McCreary.

By *Clarence A. O'Brien*

and *Harvey B. Jacobson*

Attorneys

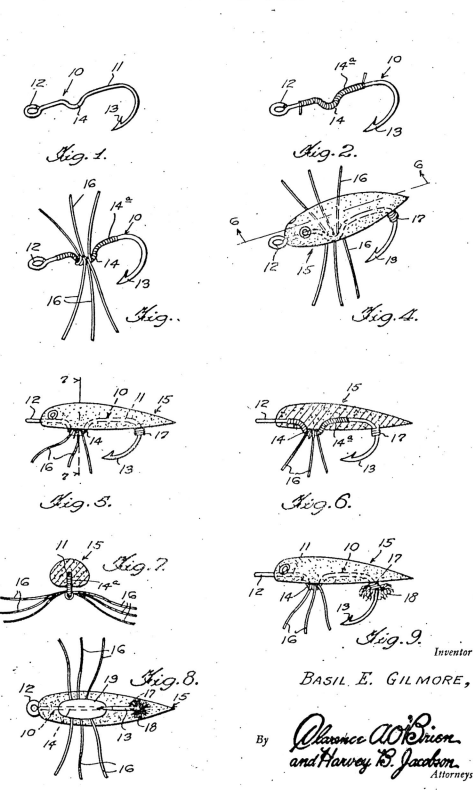

Fig. 1.

Fig. 2.

Fig. .

Fig. 4.

Fig. 5.

Fig. 6.

Fig. 7.

Fig. 8.

Fig. 9.

Inventor

BASIL E. GILMORE,

By Clarence A. O'Brien
and Harvey B. Jacobson
Attorneys

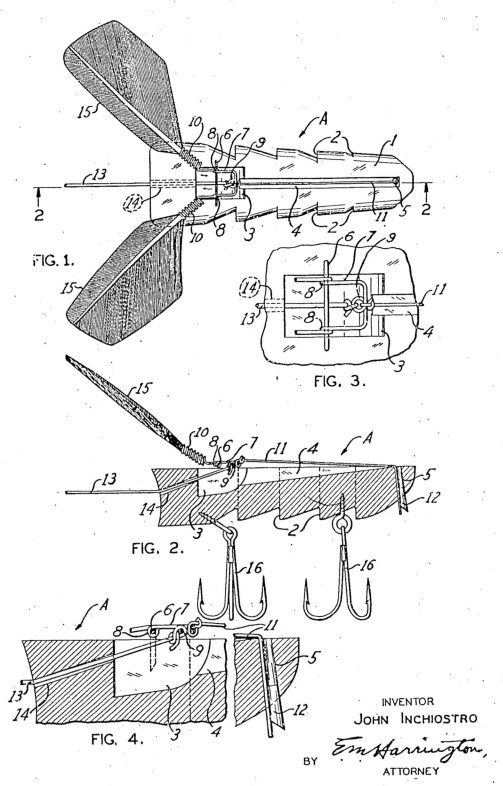

FIG. 1.

FIG. 3.

FIG. 2.

FIG. 4.

INVENTOR

JOHN INCHIOSTRO

BY Em Harrington,

ATTORNEY

Sept. 20, 1949.   L. L. BRANDT   2,482,648

FISH LURE

Filed July 23, 1945

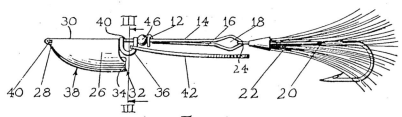

FIG. 1.

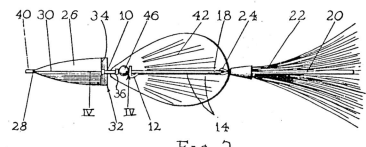

FIG. 2.

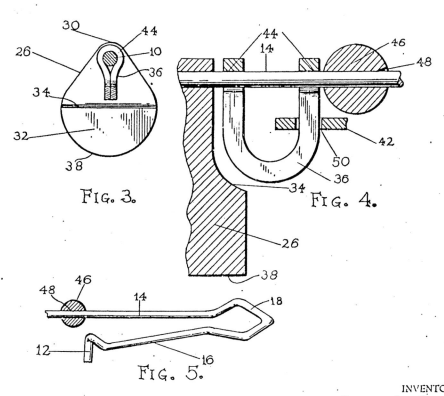

FIG. 3.   FIG. 4.

FIG. 5.

INVENTOR.
LEWIS L. BRANDT.

BY

ATTORNEY

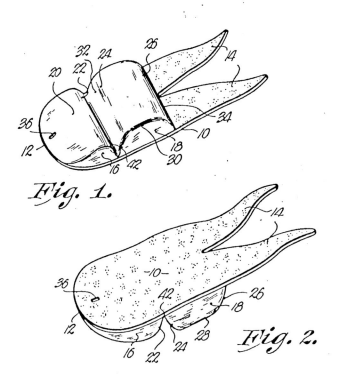

Fig. 1.

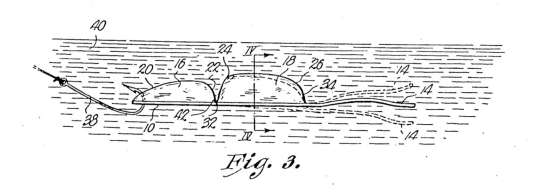

Fig. 2.

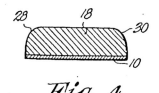

Fig. 3.

Fig. 4.

INVENTORS.
Arthur S. Lutz
Harold J. Lutz

BY

ATTORNEY

California

June 6, 1950

R. W. BERRY

2,510,769

FISHING LURE

Filed Nov. 1, 1945

Fig. 1.

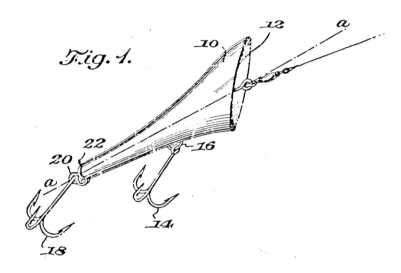

Fig. 2.

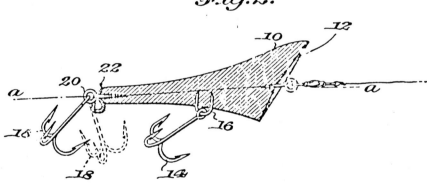

Fig. 3.

Inventor

R. W. Berry

By

Attorney

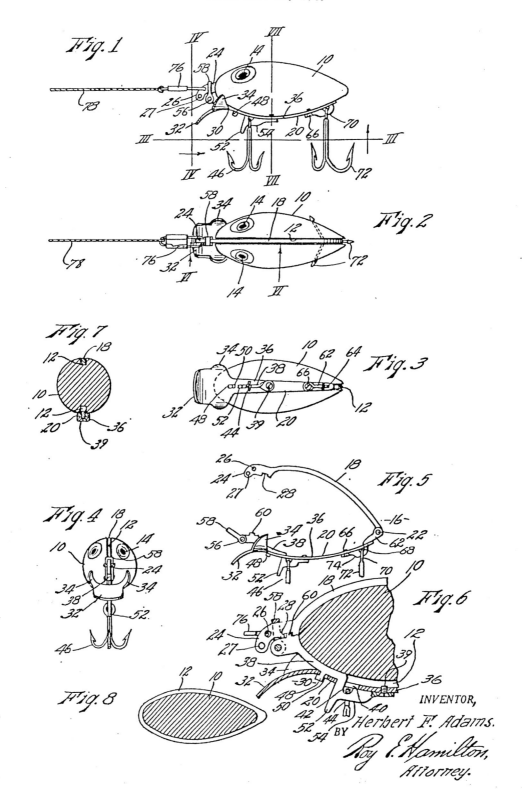

Doniphan

H. W. STEEN

2,532,961

Dec. 5, 1950

METHOD OF TYING FLIES

Filed Aug. 27, 1946

Fig.1

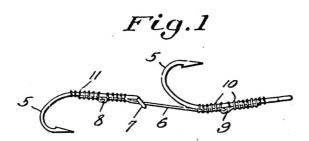

Fig.2.

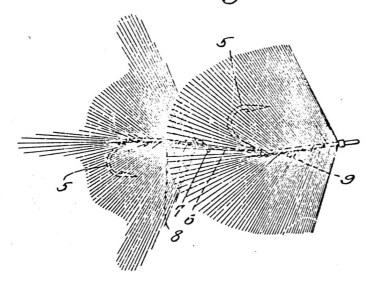

Inventor

H. W. Steen

By C.B. Knowles.

Attorneys.

July 3, 1951

St. Louis

C. MINTNER

2,559,542

FISH LURE

Filed June 2, 1948

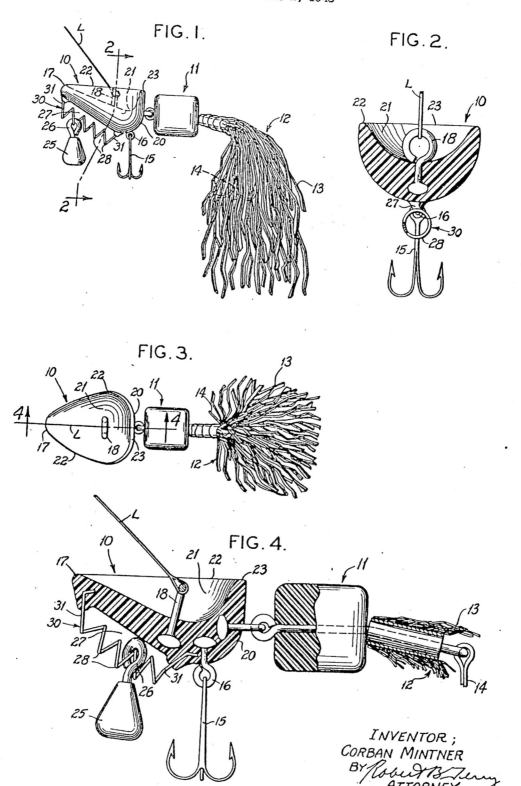

FIG. 1.

FIG. 2.

FIG. 3.

FIG. 4.

INVENTOR;
CORBAN MINTNER
BY Robert B. Terry
ATTORNEY

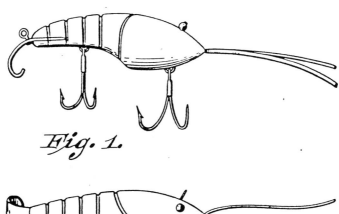

Fig. 1.

Fig. 2.

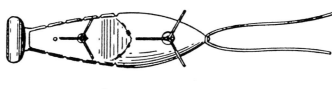

Fig. 3.

Fig. 4.

Fig. 5.

INVENTOR.
Hubert R. Smith

BY

ATTORNEY.

93

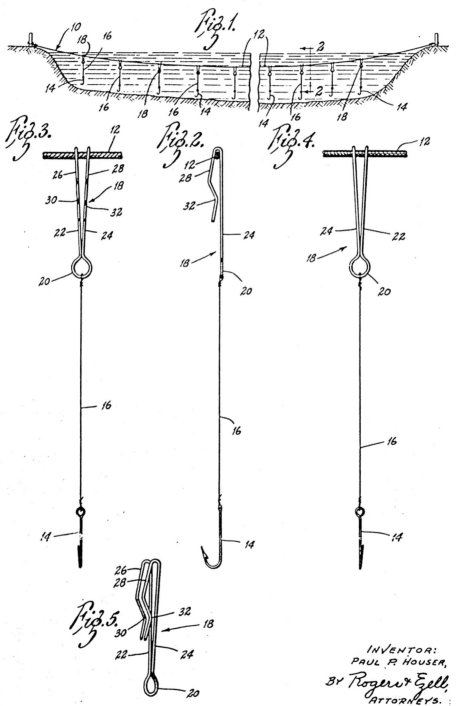

INVENTOR:
PAUL P. HOUSER,
BY Rogers & Ezell,
ATTORNEYS.

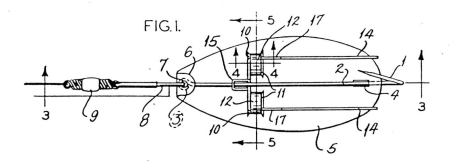

FIG. 1.

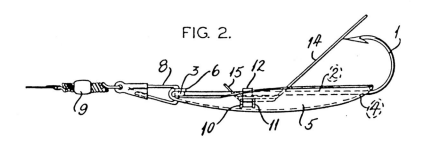

FIG. 2.

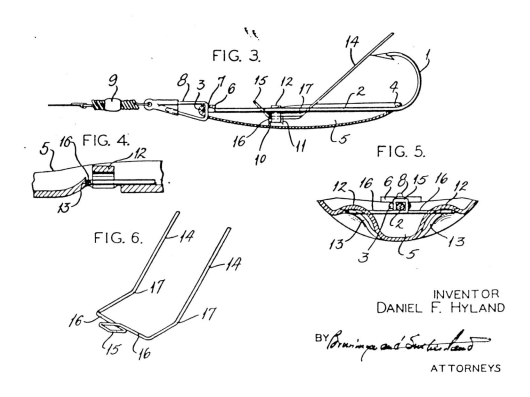

FIG. 3.

FIG. 4.

FIG. 5.

FIG. 6.

INVENTOR
DANIEL F. HYLAND

BY

ATTORNEYS

95

March 4, 1952

Kansas City

C. O. SMITH

2,588,300

ARTIFICIAL FISHING BAIT

Filed Aug. 4, 1949

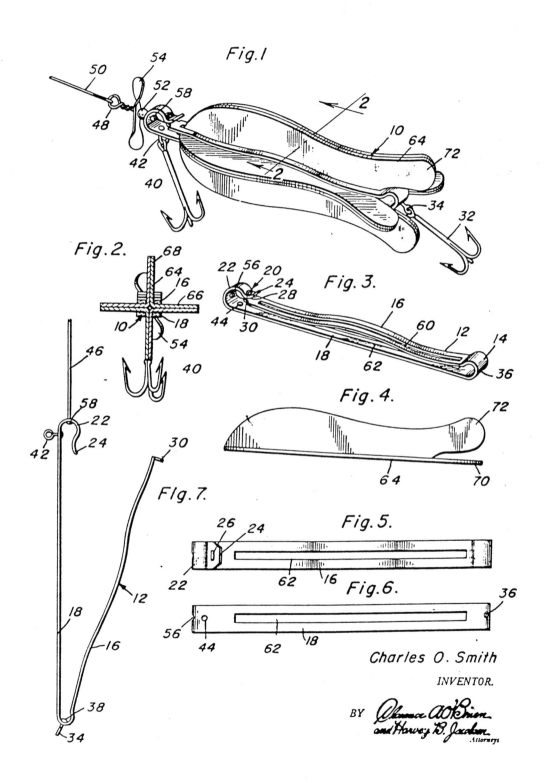

Fig.1

Fig.2.

Fig.3.

Fig.4.

Fig.7.

Fig.5.

Fig.6.

Charles O. Smith

INVENTOR.

BY

Attorneys

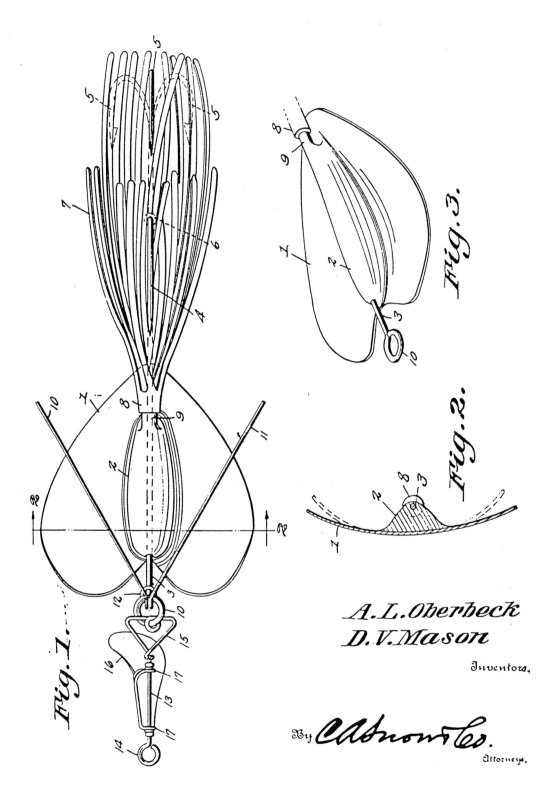

Fig. 1 · *Fig. 2.* · *Fig. 3.*

A.L.Oberbeck
D.V.Mason

Inventors,

By CASnow Co.

Attorneys.

Windsor

July 5, 1955

W. M. ALLEN

2,712,196

FLY LINE TERMINAL ANCHOR

Filed July 15, 1954

FIG.1.

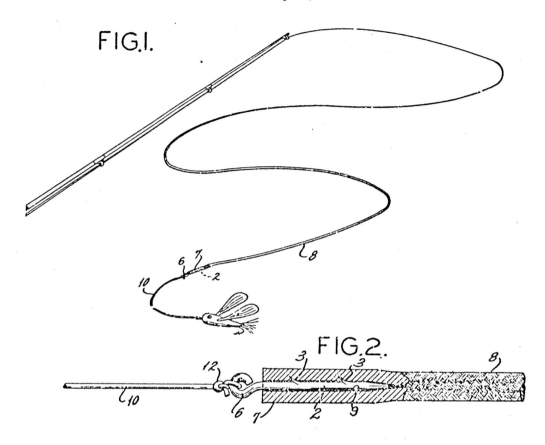

FIG.2.

FIG.3.

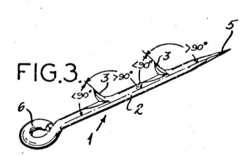

INVENTOR
WESLEY M. ALLEN
By Philip B. Polster
ATTORNEY

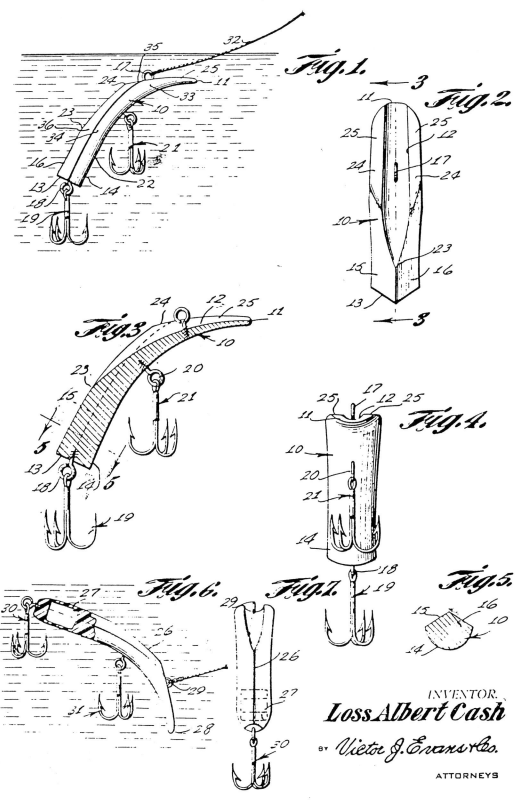

INVENTOR.
Loss Albert Cash

BY *Victor J. Evans & Co.*

ATTORNEYS

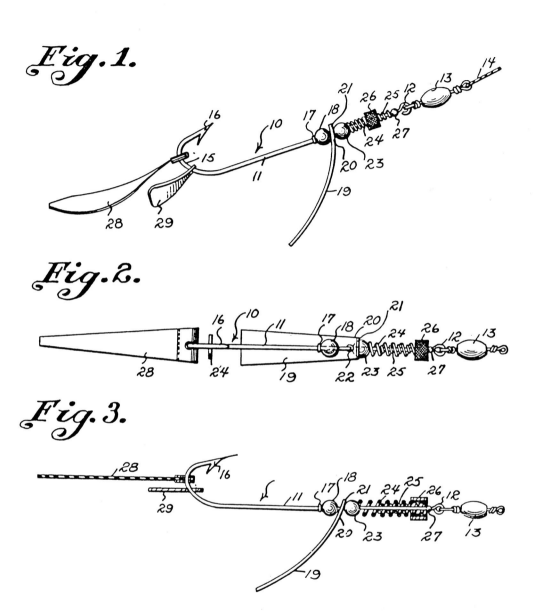

Fig. 1.

Fig. 2.

Fig. 3.

INVENTOR.
Frank C. Pollard
BY Victor J. Evans & Co.

ATTORNEYS

100

July 15, 1952

Palmyra

F. C. POLLARD

2,603,024

FISHING LURE

Filed May 29, 1947

2 SHEETS—SHEET 2

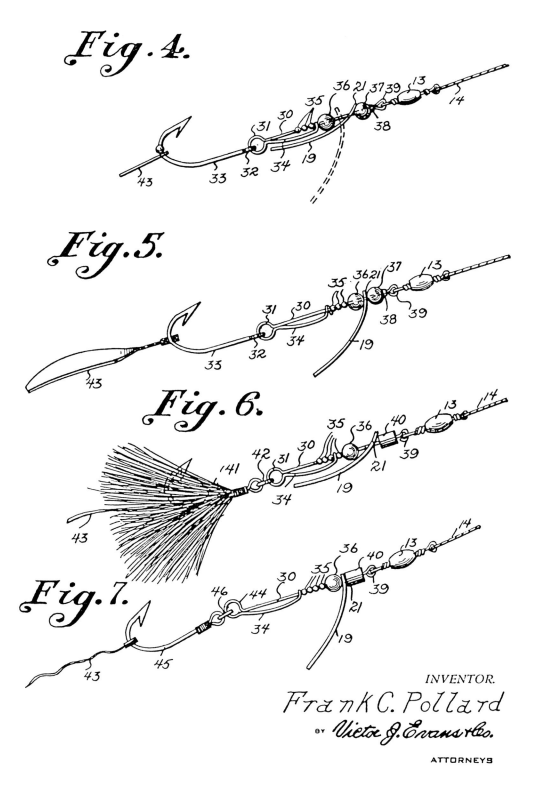

Fig.4.

Fig.5.

Fig.6.

Fig.7.

INVENTOR.

Frank C. Pollard

BY Victor J. Evans & Co.

ATTORNEYS

101

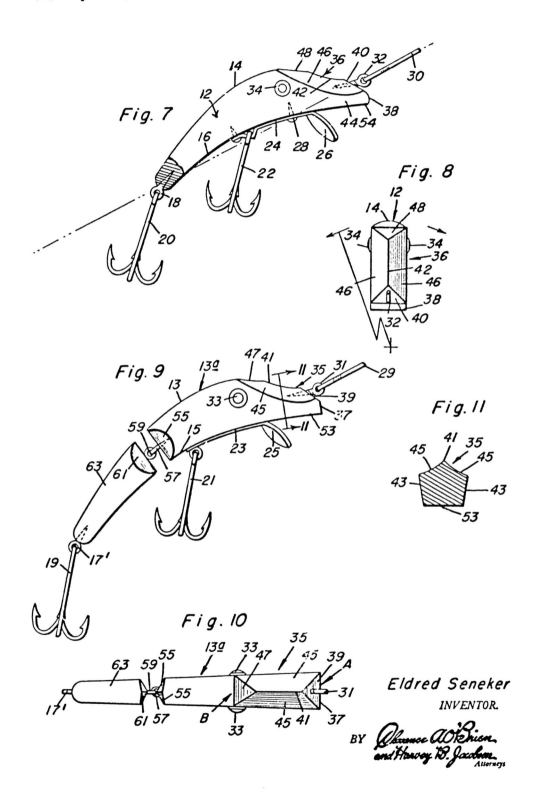

Fig. 7

Fig. 8

Fig. 9

Fig. 11

Fig. 10

Eldred Seneker
INVENTOR.

BY
Attorneys

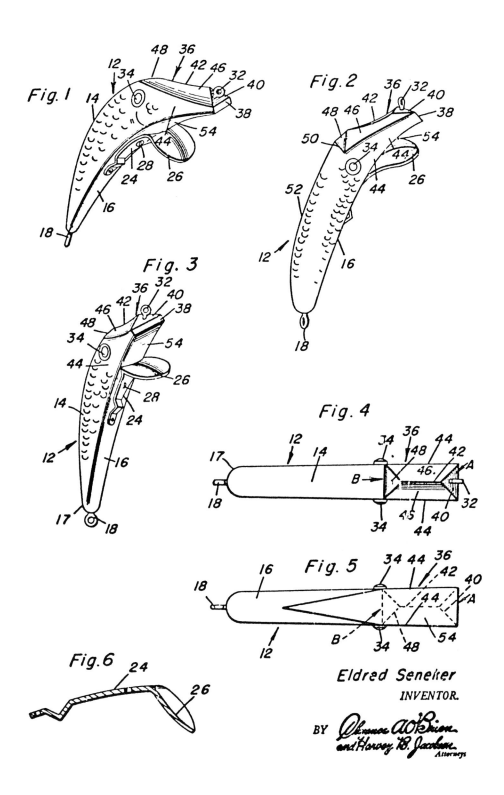

Eldred Seneker
INVENTOR.

BY *Vernon A. O'Brien*
and Harvey B. Jackson
Attorneys

Fig. 1

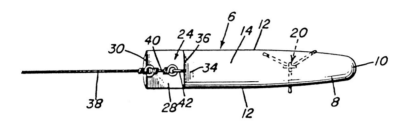

Fig. 2

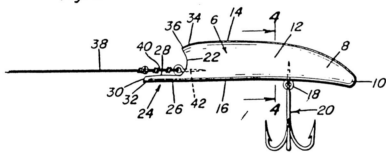

Fig. 3

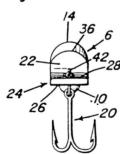

Fig. 4

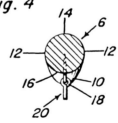

Paul L. Baker
INVENTOR.

BY *Clarence A. O'Brien*
and Harvey B. Jacobson
Attorneys

104

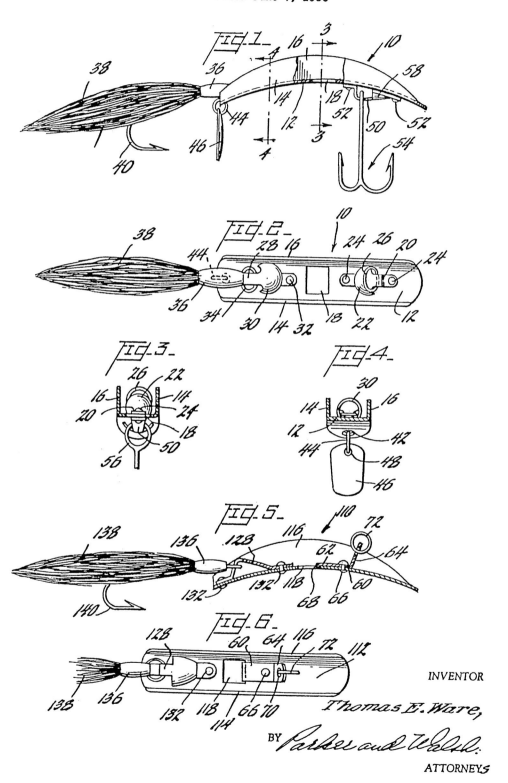

INVENTOR

Thomas E. Ware,

BY Parker and Walsh.

ATTORNEYS

105

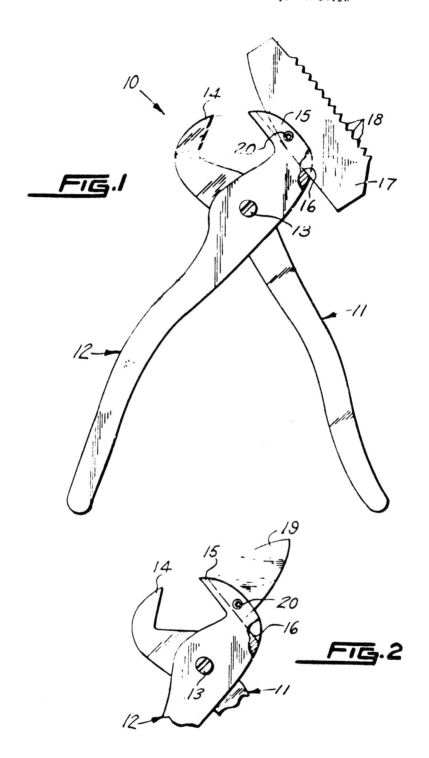

FIG.1

FIG.2

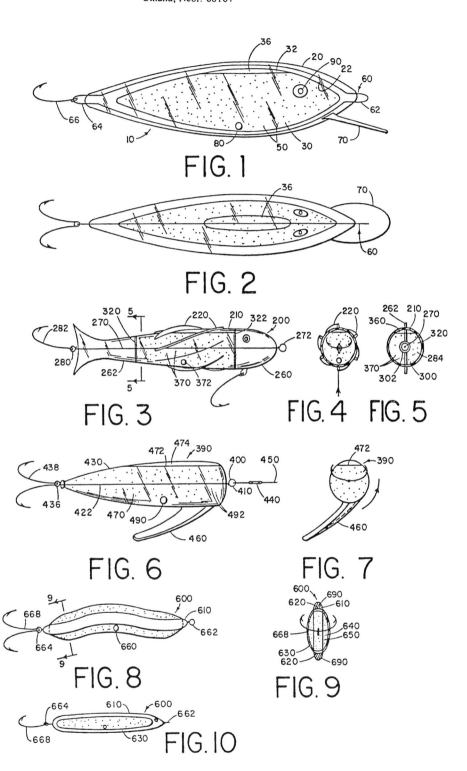

FIG. 1

FIG. 2

FIG. 3   FIG. 4   FIG. 5

FIG. 6   FIG. 7

FIG. 8   FIG. 9

FIG. 10

LIPMAN LURES, Inc.

Manufacturers of BIG-EYE LURES

2528 Dodier   St. Louis 7, Mo.   CEntral 4990

CHARLES M. SIX TACKLE CO.
TRIED AND PROVEN FISHING LURES
CARTHAGE, MISSOURI

MADE IN U. S. A.

Ozark Mountain Tackle Co.   Order Form

DATE _____   SHIP DATE _____
STORE NAME_____
ADDRESS_____
CITY/ST. _____   ZIP_____
TERMS _____   PO #_____

COLOR	2/8	1/2	2/4	B/G	PAN	PAN-JR	WW	WW-JR	WP	POP-EYE	KF

Swamp Fox Lures, Inc.
429 SALCEDO ROAD
SIKESTON, MISSOURI 63801

MOSS BOSS

Owner
ALBERT (ROY) MARKS— PH. 314-471-55

THE JUDGE'S JAW BREAKER

A Wig-Wagging-Wiggler

If fish are hungry they'll bite it — If not they'll fight it

Marlynn
LURE CO.

LITTON TACKLE COMPANY

821 NORTH MILL STREET   FESTUS, MISSOURI

MAKERS OF
"LURES WITH FISH APPEAL."

HOME
OF
QUALITY TACKLE
"BUILT TO TAKE IT"

"for efficiency in fishing"

FLIES
FLY ROD PLUGS
CASTING PLUGS
LINE DRESSING
SPINNERS

INVOICE

Berry-Lebeck Manufacturing Company

Manufacturers of Fine Fishing Lures

California, Missouri. U. S. A.

OZARKA LURE

A great fish catcher . . . .

FOR SPINNING, CASTING AND TROLLING

 LURES

Sensational NEW Development
for Spin Fishing!

3606 WOODLAND AVENUE

KANSAS CITY 9, MISSOURI

Wilson-Allen W/A Corporation

BOX 64, 113 E. BENTON ● WINDSOR, MISSOURI, 65
TELEPHONE 816-647-3125

COMPLETE SPINNER LINE   WORLD WIDE JOBBER DISTRIBUTION WRITE FOR CATALOG

McDonald—ON THE FARM

REFERENCES

American Business Directories
5711 South 86th Circle,
Omaha, NE 68127

Barzee, Ray and Jim Bourdon 1948
The Water Scout and Other Clark Baits.
Jim Bourdon, Nordica Dr., Croton-on-Hudson,
NY 10520

Luckey, Carl F. 1991
Old Fishing Lures and Tackle.
Books Americana, P.O. Box 2326, Florence,
AL 35630

Smith, Larry 1990
Great Tackle Advertisements 1874-1955.
Larry Smith, 2295 Woody Knoll Drive, Portage, MI 49002

Spink, Charles 1948
The Sporting Goods Dealers Directory.
The Sporting Goods Publ. Co., St. Louis, MO

Streater, Richard L. 1987
Streater's Reference Catalog of Old Fishing Tackle.
Richard Streater, Mercer Island, WA 98040

White, Karl T. 1990
Fishing Tackle Antiques and Collectibles.
Karl T. White, P.O. Box 9, Luther, OK 73054

INDEX

-A-

Able 2 Products 51
Alexander's Angling Products 51
Alron Lures 51
Anderson Bait Co. 16
    ABC Lure
Andrews Lure Co. 34
AR-CO-MO 16
    Hornet Sr.
    Hornet Jr.
Arnold Mfg. Co 1
    Casting Weight
Atomic Bait Co 34

-B-

B & F Mfg. Co. 16
Baker's Impy Lure Co, ... 17
    Impy Lure
    Impy Lure Jr.
Balsa Baits Company 35
    Balsa Boogie
Bass Napper Manufacturing, ... 51
Bass Buster 33
Battlefield Wire Products 35
Bee-Jay Co. 51
Berry-LeBeck Mfg. Co. 17
    Talky Topper
    200 Series Wee Gee
    300 Series Wee Gee
Cal Biddlecome Bait Mfg. Co. 18
    Cal's Crippled Minnow
Biddlecome Fly Co. 18
Biddlecome-Six Tackle Co, ... 19
    Toppy Popper
Blakemore Lure Company 35, 51
    Roadrunners and Jigs
Enoch Buchanan 46
    Homemade lures
Butler Bros. 52

-C-

Carnival Cork Co. 19
    Cork and line on card
Carter Carburetor Lure 46
    Homemade Lure
Central Molding and Mfg. Co. 19
    Plastic float
Century Plastic Co. 19
    Gee Gee Glo Worm
Champ-Items, Inc. 40

Charmer Minnow Co. 2
    Charmer Minnow
    Surface Charmer
C. A. Clark Mfg. Co. 6
    Water Scout
    Jointed Scout
    Little Eddie
    Duckbill
    Duckling
    Streamliner
    Popper Scout
    Top Scout
    Goofy Gus
    Dwarf Deamon
Charlie Coatney 35
    Spinner baits and jigs
E. E. Coombs 7
Cooper Enterprises 40
    Little-Jul
    Little-Jul Jr.
Courtney Spec. Co. 19
    Deep Diver
F. B. Cravens 8
    Flies
Culver Lures Co. 8
    Sim's Killer Lure
    Fly Maker's Manual

-D-

Danon Co. 40
    Light Emitting Plug
Bill Debo 46
    Homemade lures
Diamond Mfg. Co. 2
    Spinners
    Casting Line
Rube Dick 47
    Homemade Ozark Ike
Dickson Clawson Co. 40
    Red cedar tackle box
D. B. Doty Inc. 20
    Doty Raider
Duble The Katch Tackle Co. 41
    Minnow rig

-E-

Early Bird Baits 51
E. Eaton 47
    Homemade lures
Elliott Arms Co. 52

Ernie Enfield 47
    Homemade Ozark Ike
Ted Eudy 48
    Homemade lures

-F-

Falcon Products, Inc. 20
W. W. Faris Mfg. Co. 20
    Worm bucket
    Minnow bucket
Fetchi Lure Co. 21
    Lizard
    Popeye
Fisherman's Fly and Tackle Co. ...41
    Aero Spinner
Fisherman's Supply Co. 2
Flexilure Co. 21
    Flex-minnow
Fly Boy Lures 41
    Fly Boy
H. Fritschen 48
    Homemade lure
Henry Fuller 41

-G-

Gateway Sporting Goods 52
Gilmore Tackle Co. 9
    Gillie Streamer Flies
    Popping bugs
Glozier Mfg. Co. 35
Gourmet Lures, Inc. 41
    Captive Catch
Gray's Lazy Hooker 51
J. F. Gregory 3
    Magic Fish Lure
Guy Lure Co. 41
    Raider Jr.

-H-

H & K Sales Co. 22
Ham's Dry Line 35
Hawg-Jaw Tackle & Supply 51
Hawk Fish Lure Co. 22
    Bass Hawk ....
    Bayou Boogie
    Bombadier
Heluva Lure Corp. 51
Bill Herington Bait Co. 10
    Bag O Mad
    Bag O Mad Jr.
Mike Hildreth 22
    Wonder Bug
Houser Fly Co. 23
    Loudmouth

Hutchins Tackle.............................35

-I-

International Metal Products Co. ..24

-J-

J-D Lures Co. 42
J. & Jay Bait Co............................42
Jax Auto Float Co. 24
    Auto hooking float
Jewel Industries 51
Johnson Fishing, Inc. 51
Johnny's Jig Co. 42
Judge's Bait Shop 24
    Judge's Jaw Breaker

-K-

K-S Mfg. Co. 36
    Kitchen Sink
Kennard Mfg. Co...........................25

-L-

Laker...51
Landon Laboratories 25
    Getzem Fish-bite Bait
Lange Lure Co. 42
Gene Larew Company 36
Don Latta 36
    Honey Bee
Leacock Sporting Goods Co. 52
    Fly fishing tackle
Le-Ber Co. 36
Leslie Lure Co. 42
Liberty Outdoors, Inc. 25, 51
Liberty Mfg. Co............................25
    Darting Lizard
Lipman Lures, Inc. 25
    Lippy's Big Eye
    Whamee
Litton Tackle Co............................11
    Irresistible Bass Bait
    Flies
Lotz Brothers 52
Lucky Strike Mfg. 36, 51
Lur-Ozark Co., Inc. 26
Earl Lutes 48
    Homemade lures
Lutz Pork Bait Co...........................1
    Pork rind baits

-M-

Magnetic Fish Bait Co. 3
McClean's Sporting Goods 52
McDonald Manufacturing Company ... 11
    King Crawdad
    Flyrod spinners
    Merry Minnow
The Marc Reel Co. 26
    Marc Reel
MarLynn Lure Co. 26, 51
    Reaper Spoon
    Gold Bug
    Thing-Ma-Jig
May Fly Co. 12
    Fly fishing tackle
Metro Specialty 37
    Glitter Gitter
Midwest Pegboard Co. 42
Midwest Sales 42
Miller Lure Co. 27
    Topkick
    Topkick Jr.
Missouri Bait Co. 3
    Mizzouri Bug Wabbler
Missouri Lures, Ltd. 27
    Emory's Lure
Mitey Mite Lure Co. 27
Montavy Bait Co. 28
    Big Bop
Moore Fishing Enterprises, Inc. 51
Mueller-Perry Co. 28
    Crazy Legs

-N-

Natural Fly Co. 12
Naturalure Bait Co. 4
    Flyrod popping bugs
Nature Faker Lures, Inc. 28
    Shammy Strip
    Plastic grasshopper
    No Knot Eyelet
Newton Mfg. & Sales Co. 42
    Newton Comet Spoon
Norkin Laboratories 42
    The Fluke

-O-

Owensville Sporting Goods, Inc. ..42
The Ozark Bait Co. (California) 12
    The Shiek
Ozark Bait Co. (Windsor) 43
    Paul's Pal
Ozark Bait Co. (Joplin) 43

Ozark Mountain Tackle Co. 37
    Woodchopper
    Woodpopper
    Woodwalker

-P-

P & H Bait Co. 29
    Ripple Tail
Paugh Fly Shop 29
Perfection Bait Co. 4
Phantom Products, Inc. 29
Piney River Bass Flies 43
    Flies
J. A. Plasters Co. 13
    Ideal Trotline Clips
Playmore Products, Inc. 29
Prairie Hollow Tackle Co. 51
Presto Knocker Co. 43
    Presto Knocker
Noel A. Price Co. 51

-R-

R. B. S. Lure Co. 44
    Van De Reit's Spoon
Rainbow Lures 51
Rawlings Sporting Goods 52
Ray-Lee Tackle 51
Reflex Specialties Co., Inc. 30
Richards and Conover 53
Rieadco Corporation 51
Jim Rogers Lures 51
    Craw-Pap

-S-

Self-striking Fish Cork Co. 4
Semo Tackle Co. 37
E. T. Senseney 30
Shallow Water Bait Co. 49
    Blooper
    Frog
    Varment
    Lazy Minnow
Shapleigh Hardware Co. 53
Shiloh Lure Company 51
C. A. Shores 38
    Fish Napper
Show-me Wooden Classics 49
    Nick's Zip Stick
Simmons Hardware Co. 53

Charles M. Six Co. 30
    Six's Special
    Skipper
    Little Suzy
    Little Teaz
Skipper Bait Co. 38
    Moss King
Smith Bros. 49
    Homemade Ozark Ike
B. G. Smith Co. 31
    The Shark
Smith & Yelton Co. 31
    Smitty's Crawpappy
Soft Pak U S A 51
  Split Cork Float 13
    Cork Float
Springfield Novelty Co. 14
    Reel Lure
    1/2 Charmer
    Hollow-head
Spurgeon Lures 44
    Crooked Hooker
Howard W. Steen 14
    Double Flies
    Homemade Lure
E. S. Stofer Mfg. Co. 44
Stoner Machine & Mfg. Co. 44
    Lucky Twister
Stream Sweeper Lures 32
    Homemade Lure
Strike-it, Inc. 32
    Plastic Pork Rind
Strike Zone Lures 51
Structure Lure Co. 44
Super Products Co. 32
    Hook-n-Lure Retriever
Swamp Fox Lures 38
    Moss Boss

-T-

Talbot Reel & Mfg. Co. 4
    Talbot Reels
Taneycomo Fish Bait Co. 15
W. C. Taylor 15
    Flyrod Frog
Tee Cee Tackle 51
Three J Bait Co. 44
Thulco Products 44
    D-Thing Hook Retriever
Triumph Mfg. Co. 39

The Turner Co. 33
    Spider Lure

-U-

Ultra Lure 45
Unknown 50
    Homemade Lures

-V-

V. J. Lure Co. 39
Art Varner Fly Co. 45
    Flies

-W-

William G. Wade 50
    Homemade Lures
Wally R. Lure Co. 45
    Sting Ray
Walton Supply Co. 54
The Ward Co. 33
    Homemade Lure
Tom Ware Fishing Tackle Co. 33
    Fly Plug
J. A. Wavrin 5
Willey-J-Bait Co. 45
Wilson-Allen Corp. 34, 51
    No-Knot Eyelet
Clinton Wilt Mfg. Co. 5
    Champion
    Little Wonder
Witte Hardware Co. 54
Woodchip & Sawdust Shop 49
    Homemade Lures
Wyeth Co. 54

-Y-

Young Manufacturing Company ... 51

-Z-

K. C. Zumwalt Co. 45
    Swivel Sinkers